The Perfect Prescription for Life's Many Crises

C*cktail THERAPY

Leanne Shear &
Tracey Toomey

Illustrated by Neryl Walker

SSE

SIMON SPOTLIGHT ENTERTAINMENT

NEW YORK   LONDON   TORONTO   SYDNEY

S|S|E

SIMON SPOTLIGHT ENTERTAINMENT
An imprint of Simon & Schuster
1230 Avenue of the Americas, New York, New York 10020
Text copyright © 2007 by Leanne Shear and Tracey Toomey
Illustrations copyright © 2007 by Neryl Walker/
www.artscounselinc.com.

SIMON SPOTLIGHT ENTERTAINMENT and related logo
are trademarks of Simon & Schuster, Inc.
Designed by Jane Archer
Manufactured in the United States of America
First Edition 10 9 8 7 6 5 4 3 2
Library of Congress Cataloging-in-Publication Data
Shear, Leanne.
Cocktail therapy / by Leanne Shear and Tracey Toomey ;
illustrated by Neryl Walker.
p. cm.
Includes bibliographical references and index.
ISBN-13: 978-1-4169-4836-0
ISBN-10: 1-4169-4836-8
1. Cocktails. I. Toomey, Tracey. II. Title.
TX951.S52 2007
641.8'74—dc22
2007010147
www.SimonSaysTheSPOT.com

Leanne and Tracey wish to thank: Our fabulous agent, Elisabeth Weed at Trident Media, who is not only *always* in our corner but also an incredibly astute businesswoman, creative mind, and great friend; our fantastic and talented editor, Emily Westlake, who made this whole process the incredibly fun learning experience that it was; all of our eclectic friends, new and old, who make the process of life enjoyable!

Leanne wishes to thank: As with everything I do in my life, this wouldn't be possible without the love and support of my mom, Lynn Erickson, and sister, Molly Shear, as well as the rest of my huge and happy clan, and all of my friends. I count my blessings every day!

Tracey wishes to thank: My hubby and love of my life, Matt. Thanks to you, I no longer have to refer to the Romantic Minefields section of this book! My mom, dad, Kerry, and Jack—

thank you for your tireless support and infinite enthusiasm about everything I do. And to all my girls who have generously shared their crises (and favorite cocktails!) so that we could complete this book.

Table of Contents

Introduction

Ｐeople love to spill their guts to the person who pours their pint. After all, the bartender is the most accessible— and cheapest!—therapist around. When we first started bartending, we had no idea how to handle our *own* personal catastrophes, much less diffuse other people's. But after years of enduring slammed nights behind the bar (where we commiserated with countless customers), we began doling out advice on a regular basis. Along the way, we discovered that there's a cocktail suited for each and every calamity. So while some people take refuge on the racquetball court or with a good cry, we've concluded that the quickest way to banish the blues is with a delicious drink. And we're ready to spill (advice, not drinks, that is).

These days, the more innovative and inspired cocktails are, the better. The liquor industry is booming with more and more liquor brands and flavors popping up all the time, and along with our fellow mixologists, we've taken note. When we're behind the bar in Manhattan's trendy SoHo district or in the Hamptons, it's imperative that we craft cocktails not only with a splash of creativity, but also with a twist of style and sophistication. Naturally, being the classic-cocktail aficionados that we are, we set out to prove that not all drinks should be fluorescent pink, super sugary sweet, or served with a tiny paper umbrella, and in doing so, we joined the cocktail renaissance sweeping the country. Our cocktails are liquid culinary works of art, made with freshly squeezed juices, fruit purees, and fresh herbs. Gone are the days of syrupy, hangover-inducing sour mixes and lime juice out of the bottle! Here, in addition to prescribing the perfect drink for any situation, we offer quick and easy technical advice that will make any amateur look like a cocktail connoisseur, allowing readers everywhere to tap into the growing trend of the sophisticated cocktail, long considered to be the ideal antidote to all of life's crises!

We've organized the book according to the severity and type of predicament you might find yourself in (you won't be surprised to learn that the section dealing with all things romantic— "Romantic Minefields"—was so crisis-laden, we had to break it up into subsections!), so even in a panic-ridden state, you'll be able to quickly and effortlessly flip the page and find the drink to cure your ill. That hot guy you met last week still hasn't called? Try a Pomegranate Martini—bold, tasty, but not so lethal that you'll be tempted to drunk dial him. The dry cleaner shrunk your favorite pants (or, worse, you've put on a few pounds)? Indulge in a (nearly) guiltless Sugar-Free Mojito. Credit card bill contained a few nasty surprises? A decadent Bourbon Bee Sting will leave you feeling like a million dollars. Or perhaps you "accidentally" came across an incriminating e-mail exchange between your boyfriend and his sexy coworker? We have just the drink to mix with your tears. Whatever the crisis, we prescribe the perfect cocktail to help you get back on your feet, back at your ex, or back in the game.

Cheat Sheet

Before we start doling out drinks, it's useful to go back to the basics. Once you've gotten these down, nothing can come between you and your cocktail cure. The following will provide any at-home bartender with tricks of the trade to help you master the perfect drink for every imperfect situation.

The "Simplest" Simple Syrup: What's known in the biz as "simple syrup" is the bartender's secret ingredient. The sugar is fully dissolved, so it evenly distributes sweetness to cocktails without making them grainy. Simple syrup can be used to sweeten everything from iced tea to Mint Juleps.

>1 cup granulated sugar
>
>$\frac{1}{2}$ cup water

In a small saucepan, heat the sugar and water and bring to a boil, stirring occasionally. When the sugar is completely dissolved, remove from heat and cool to room temperature. Refrigerate, covered, for up to one week.

Ginger Syrup: This is great for a Ginger Ginseng Martini or your own creative concoction.

>Zest of 1 lemon
>
>2 cups coarsely chopped fresh ginger with peel (about 8 ounces)
>
>1 cup sugar
>
>2 cups water

Remove the outer peel of the lemon with a zester, grater, or vegetable peeler, taking care not to include too much of the bitter white pith. Finely chop the lemon peel and ginger in a food processor. Transfer the lemon-ginger mixture to a medium saucepan, add the sugar and water, and bring to a boil. Reduce heat and simmer, partially covered, for 15 minutes. Strain the mixture and cool. Cover and refrigerate for up to one week.

Sour Mix: Sour mix is easy to make at home, and it tastes so much better than the junk that comes out of the soda gun at the bar. Plus, when you make it yourself, you can control the amount of sugar and thus the calorie content.

> Juice of 2 lemons
> Juice of 2 limes
> Simple syrup, to taste

Combine all ingredients, adding simple syrup a little at a time until you achieve desired sweetness. Ideal sour mix should be both sweet and sour.

The Perfect Pour: Most cocktails call for 1 to 2 ounces of liquor. No seasoned cocktail maker would dare use a jigger, shot glass, or measuring cup to calculate the right amount of any ingredient. Nearly all bartenders use the "counting method." If you put a speed pourer on the top of the bottle and invert it completely, every second (think: *one one hundred, two one hundred, etc.*) is roughly 1 ounce. If you can't find a speed pourer, however, it's best to measure. Otherwise, you may have one drink and quickly find yourself on your ass!

Freshly Squeezed vs. Bottled Lemon and Lime Juice: Bottled juice is loaded with sweeteners and, as a result, calories. One entire lime yields only 10 calories, so it's a much better choice for your waistline. You need to conserve all the drink calories you can to make up for the pizza you're going to devour at 3:00 a.m.!

Impressive Purees: Purees make any cocktail sophisticated, and they're easy to make at home. You'll need:

> 1 cup sugar
> 1/2 cup water
> 8 oz. frozen peaches, raspberries, strawberries, or any other frozen fruit, thawed
> 1 tsp. grated orange, lemon, or lime zest *(which makes any frozen fruit taste like it was just picked fresh off the vine!)*

Stir the sugar and water in a large saucepan over medium heat until the sugar dissolves, about 5 minutes (just like you're making simple syrup). Cool completely. Puree the peaches or berries and orange/lemon/lime zest in a blender with the sugar syrup until smooth. Strain through a fine-meshed strainer and into a bowl. Purees will keep for months if frozen or in the refrigerator for up to a week.

Bellini Bar: An original way to instantly class up a party is to serve Bellinis. It's especially fun if you set up a Bellini bar and let guests serve themselves. You'll need a couple of bottles of champagne, Prosecco, or other sparkling wine—chilled, of course. Then provide your guests with champagne flutes and an array of purees. Traditional

Bellinis are made with peach puree, but why not spice things up with other choices like raspberry, passion fruit, and pomegranate? Fill small bowls with thinly sliced strawberries, raspberries, and mint to garnish the cocktails.

Family Feuds
& Friendship Follies

et's face it: Friends and family are the
ones who are always there for you—it's
in the job description. But for the rare
times when they're the source of your angst, we have
the cocktail to get you through any predicament.
And for the even rarer occasions when you're the
one in the wrong? Well, thankfully, pride is a lot
easier to swallow when washed down with one of
our delicious concoctions!

CRISIS:

You have plans with your best friend for cocktails
and a bite to eat at a great new lounge, and you've
been looking forward to it all day. You stopped
for a mani/pedi on the way home from work
and are all geared up, wearing your cute new top
and dangly earrings. A half hour before you're
supposed to meet, however, she calls to cancel. It's
not her fault that she has to work late, but she has
a nasty tendency to drop you at the last minute!
Your best companion in this case is an Apple
Fizz—it will never disappoint you.

COCKTAIL: *Apple Fizz*

4 oz. champagne
1 oz. apple juice
Apple slice

Fill a champagne flute three quarters full of champagne, top with the apple juice, and garnish with the apple slice. After the first sip, start going through your cell phone to find the number of your most "up for anything" friend.

BONUS: Apples are a super food: rich in fiber, vitamins, and antioxidants.

CRISIS:

Your pothead little brother forgot he was supposed to pick you up from the train station. Worse, you're forced to wait outside in the cold for two hours since he can't hear his phone over the sounds of the video game he's playing. Don't get mad, get even! Make him do all the laundry you brought home—after he concocts a Surfer on Acid for you, of course.

COCKTAIL: *Surfer on Acid*

1 oz. Jägermeister
1 oz. coconut rum
Splash of pineapple juice

Shake with ice, pour into a shot glass, and shoot. It's better than shooting your brother.

CRISIS:

After six months of dating, you and your boyfriend have gotten in the habit of spending every night together. Summer rolls around and you bring him on vacation with your family. Since becoming a bona fide adult, you'd forgotten about your parents' old-fashioned no-sleeping-in-the-same-room-until-marriage dictum. What other option do you and your man have? Down a Sex on the Beach . . . and then sneak out for some sex on the beach!

COCKTAIL: *Sex on the Beach*

1 oz. premium vodka
1 oz. peach schnapps
2 oz. cranberry juice
2 oz. grapefruit juice
Lemon or lime slice

Combine all ingredients with ice and serve in
a collins glass on the rocks. Garnish with a
lemon or lime.

CRISIS:

It seems as the the years progress, you're getting exponentially closer with your mom (thank God your once-raging teenage angst is finally abating). She's your biggest fan and cheerleader, and you couldn't imagine getting through life's crises without her. Then one day you get into an enormous fight, and you both slam down the phone, leaving the issue unresolved. Take a page from the Rolling Stones' playbook: While you don't have to go as far as popping pills, you can kill the pain with a Mother's Little Helper. Soothing, calming, and warming, it's the exact opposite of how you feel post-blowup.

COCKTAIL: *Mother's Little Helper*

2 oz. dark rum
3 oz. apple cider
Pinch of cloves

Combine all ingredients in a mug and zap in the microwave to warm it up. Sip slowly, and then, just like Mom taught you all those years ago, be the bigger person and call her back to work it out . . . even if she was the one in the wrong.

BONUS: Cloves have been proven to have anesthetic and anti-inflammatory properties and to work wonders in preventing toxins from damaging your body.

CRISIS:

The truth is, if it weren't for your parents, you wouldn't be here. But just because Mom and Dad gave you life, that doesn't mean they should *micromanage* it. If you find yourself stuck listening to one of their speeches on where you should live, what job you should take, and who you should marry during a routine Sunday afternoon phone call, you have two choices: You can either get in a sour mood, or you can excuse yourself and whip up a Sour Apple Martini. If you haven't figured it out by now, we recommend the latter.

COCKTAIL: *Sour Apple Martini*

2 oz. premium vodka
1 oz. sour apple schnapps
Splash of fresh lime juice
Maraschino cherry

Combine all fluids in a shaker over ice and strain into a chilled martini glass. Garnish with a cherry. After a few sweet and sour sips, call up your parents and assert your independence. And remember: An apple martini a day keeps the parents at bay.

Crisis:

She's done it again. But this time, she got locked up. You've been bailing your little sister out of jams since before she hit puberty, and now you're her "one phone call" from jail. After springing your sister from the, ahem, slammer, really, isn't your only option an Alabama Slamma'?

COCKTAIL: *Alabama Slamma'*

$\frac{1}{2}$ oz. amaretto
$\frac{1}{2}$ oz. Southern Comfort
$\frac{1}{2}$ oz. sloe gin
Splash of orange juice
Splash of sour mix

Combine all ingredients in a shaker with ice and strain into a shot glass. If your sister's expecting you to take a second mortgage out on your house so that you can post her bail, double the recipe.

CRISIS:

It can be harder to find the perfect pair
of jeans than it is to find the perfect man,
but somehow, you found them. They're
incredible—they give your butt a lift, flatten
your tummy, and elongate your legs. And so
what if they cost more than a month's rent?
You look hot and you deserve them. But then
your roommate borrows said pair of jeans
(without asking) and proceeds to get drunk,
fall on her ass, and rip them. Since you feel
like you're going to explode, we suggest an
Irish Car Bomb. Creamy and delicious (in fact,
it tastes like a milk shake!), it will blow even
the most dour of moods to smithereens.

COCKTAIL: Irish Car Bomb

> 8 oz. Guinness
> 1 oz. Irish whiskey
> ½ oz. Irish cream liqueur

Fill a pint glass halfway with Guinness and allow the beer to settle. Pour the whiskey in a shot glass and top with the Irish cream. Drop the shot glass into the beer and chug.

 TIP JAR: (Caution: The following is a frat-boy rule, but it often applies in rowdy bars.) If you're doing Car Bombs with a lot of people, it's often standard to race and see who can gulp their drink down the fastest. The last guy to finish should—naturally—have to pay for everyone's drinks.

CRISIS:

You just found out that your best friend from college (and current roommate) is moving across the country. Not only are you now saddled with the task of finding another roommate, but you're also losing your favorite wing-woman and confidante. Your heart hurts infinitely worse than it did when your last boyfriend dumped you, so you might as well have a sweet and soothing Broken Heart.

COCKTAIL: *Broken Heart*

> 1 oz. raspberry-flavored vodka
> 1 oz. vanilla vodka
> Splash of fresh lime juice
> Splash of simple syrup
> ½ cup muddled mixed berries
> Lime wedge

In a shaker, muddle the berries, then add all other liquid ingredients. Shake with ice and pour into a rocks glass. Garnish with a lime wedge.

CRISIS:

After college all your friends opted for fast-paced, high-paying power jobs. You chose a job that was emotionally fulfilling. Lucrative, though? Not so much. Now your friends have a lot of money, while you're stuck working *several* jobs just to cover the bills. To make matters worse, your pals always want to meet up at expensive restaurants and bars, and you can't even afford a salad at these posh places. On the rare occasions when your usually generous friends fail to offer to pick up your tab, it's liquid-dinner time. We suggest a decadent (and filling!) Choco-Coffee Cooler. It's impossible to feel sorry for yourself when you're sipping something so delicious and creamy.

COCKTAIL: *Choco-Coffee Cooler*

> 1 oz. vanilla vodka
> 1 ½ oz. coffee-flavored liqueur
> 1 big scoop of chocolate ice cream
> Handful of crushed ice
> ¼ cup chocolate-covered espresso
> beans *(plus a few extra for garnish)*

Blend all ingredients in a blender until combined. Pour into a large glass and top with remaining chocolate-covered espresso beans. Yummy!

TIP JAR:
How to Score a Free Drink

Nothing is better than a freebie, but in the bar world, there are certain rules of engagement that must be followed in order to attain a complimentary cocktail.

- The cardinal rule for getting a free drink at a bar is, ironically, to *never* ask for one! If you do, the result will be just like that law of physics we learned in high school: There will be an equal and opposite reaction. In other words, you'll be charged for every single thing you order.

- Read your audience, like bartenders are trained to do: If the person slinging drinks is really busy, don't bug him or her. But if you have a moment to chat, be witty, fun, and engaging (without being a pest!)—we love to forge connections with great customers, and more often than not, that means a free drink or two.

- Tip generously. Mark our words: Bartenders have memories like elephants and simply never forget the biggest (and smallest!) tips. If you take care of us, we'll take care of you.

CRISIS:

While the rest of the grown-ups in your extended family head out to a fancy dinner, you're stuck babysitting your sister's bratty kids. Since you're not getting out of it, why not make yourself a Baby Guinness (after the rug rats are tucked safely in bed, of course)? Think of it this way: At least they're not *your* kids!

COCKTAIL: *Baby Guinness*

> 2 ½ oz. Coffee-flavored liqueur
> ½ oz. Irish cream liqueur

Pour the coffee-flavored liqueur into a rocks glass. Then add the Irish cream, pouring carefully against the side of the glass to layer the drink and give the Baby Guinness its "head."

CRISIS:

You're engaged! You have a beautiful sparkler
on your left ring finger and are starting a new
life with the man you love. You've never been
happier . . . until you're faced with the dreaded
"Meeting of the Families." Your parents
have invited his folks over for dinner, and
you're terrified that the entire evening will be
shrouded in awkwardness (and you're praying
your dad doesn't whip out the VHS tape of
your second-grade dance recital). To ensure
that this gathering goes off without a hitch
(pardon the pun!), whip up a batch of Irish
Coffees. You need a little "luck of the Irish,"
and no one can resist the creamy, sweet, warm
richness of this classic cocktail.

COCKTAIL: *Irish Coffee*

1 ½ oz. Irish whiskey
3 oz. hot coffee
2 tsp. sugar
Heavy cream

Pour whiskey into a mug and top with coffee. In a shaker, combine sugar and heavy cream. Shake like crazy until you get a nice, thick whipped cream that you can spoon on top of the coffee mixture; but don't overshake or you'll end up with sweetened butter!

P.S. Hide any incriminating VHS tapes and take down that "Freshman Fifteen" photo of you that your mom has hanging on the living room wall.

Romantic Minefields

As bartenders, we've been privy to everything from cringe-worthy blind dates to couples arguing over the terms of their pre-nup. When it comes to romance, we've seen it all—the good (proposals at the bar), the bad (a girl drunkenly stalking her ex while he was on a date with a new woman), and the ugly (match.com mixers—need we say more?). So here's a recap. And after that, a nightcap!

Butterflies in Your Stomach

Nothing is more fun than the "pre-relationship relationship" (even if it exists only in your head). Cocktails offer just the liquid courage you need to turn a mere fantasy into reality. And if it doesn't work out, a tasty libation can help boost your spirits and give you the strength you need to go out and find someone new.

CRISIS:

Last week you met the hottest guy you've ever seen, and you really hit it off. Future husband alert . . . except for the pesky little fact that even though you gave him your cell phone number, office number, and three e-mail addresses, he hasn't gotten in touch with you yet. You can keep telling yourself he's just playing it cool, *Swingers*-style, but instead of brooding (and checking your e-mail and voice mail every five seconds), why not grab your girls and head out to a hot spot for some Pomegranate Martinis? They're bold and tasty but not too strong—after all, the last thing you want is to get smashed and call *him*!

COCKTAIL: Pomegranate Martini

> 3 oz. premium vodka
> 2 oz. pomegranate juice
> Pomegranate seeds

Shake vodka and juice over ice and serve straight up in a chilled martini glass. Garnish with the pomegranate seeds.

BONUS: Drink up not only because it tastes delicious, but because pomegranates are ridiculously high in antioxidants and good for your heart. How convenient!

TIP JAR:
Laws of Attraction

....

HOW TO PICK UP A GUY AT A BAR

- **Divide and Conquer**: Men often gripe to us about women who hang out in groups. It's a lot more intimidating for guys to approach a pack of girls clustered at the bar than two friends sitting at a bar. As one guy said, "I'll pass on the sorority meeting."

- **Skip the Whine**: Commiserating about, say, evil bosses can seem like a good get-to-know-you tactic, but it drags down a first encounter. Talk about something positive and you'll be smiling. *That's* irresistible.

- **Beware of Bar Slime**: A good friend of ours kept sleeping with a guy she'd see at our bar who never bothered to ask her to dinner. She insisted he'd "come around," but he never did. Wait until he asks you out on a real date before taking it to the next level. And sorry, but watching the Knicks game with his friends does *not* count as a real date.

- **Send That Guy a Drink!** Recently, a woman sitting alone at our bar ordered two guys a round of beers. They were so impressed by her boldness, they invited her to join them. Now she's seriously dating one of them. In our experience, confidence trumps all, so why not make the first move? If he's interested, he'll come to you; if not, his loss. And all it cost you was the price of a drink!

CRISIS:

Nothing—and we mean nothing—kills the mood faster than a condom breaking. The only solution is calming down with a Ginger Ginseng Martini. Both the ginger (which settles your stomach) and the ginseng (which increases the body's positive response to stress) will be the perfect companions when you head out for that pregnancy test!

COCKTAIL: *Ginger Ginseng Martini*

> 3 oz. premium vodka
> ½ oz. ginger syrup *(see "Cheat Sheet")*
> 1 ginseng tablet
> Splash of fresh lime juice
> Thin slice of fresh ginger

Crush ginseng tablet and dissolve in ginger syrup, then mix all ingredients in a shaker with ice. Serve straight up in a chilled martini glass. Garnish with a thin slice of fresh ginger.

CRISIS:

You had an amazing night out with your girlfriends, but you went a little overboard on the cocktails. What you don't remember until the next morning—when you look at the Outgoing Calls list on your phone—is that somewhere around 3:00 a.m., you got a little lonely and called your crush . . . twelve times. The only dam to stop the wave of shame washing over you is a Bloody Mary over brunch with the same evil friends from the night before. Just don't drink too much because the only thing worse than 3:00 a.m. stalker-ish booty calls are 1:00 p.m. stalker-ish booty calls!

Cocktail Therapy

COCKTAIL: *Bloody Mary*

    2 oz. premium vodka
    2 oz. tomato or vegetable juice
    Splash of Worcestershire sauce
    Splash of hot sauce
    Dollop of horseradish
    Salt and pepper, to taste
    Celery stalk

Mix everything together in a highball glass with ice. Garnish with a celery stalk. ("Stalk" being the operative word!) Hand your cell phone over to your most trustworthy friend.

 TIP JAR: Freshly squeezed tomato juice and freshly grated horseradish will really take this drink to the next level. Feel the burn, baby!

TIP JAR:
How to Avoid the Perils of Drunk Dialing

• The geniuses at Virgin Mobile now offer a booty-call-proof service. You just call a Virgin hotline, enter the number(s) you want to make sure you don't call that night, and then you're automatically blocked from making calls to those numbers until 6:00 a.m., by which point you'll hopefully be passed out next to an empty pizza box.

• If you're not a "Virgin," write down the "dangerous numbers" programmed into your phone, give the piece of paper to your best friend, then erase them from your phone.

• Don't drink. (Ha!)

CRISIS:

Remember when you first got your period and you were too mortified to even utter the word "tampon," much less be seen in public purchasing a box of Tampax? But then you grew up and got over it, right? Right. Until fifteen years later, when you're strolling through the drugstore carrying a plastic basket filled with maxi-pads, a little bottle of Beano, Bikini Zone, and Pepto-Bismol to boot, and you suddenly run into the guy you just started dating. He now knows all your dirty little secrets, so in lieu of running into aisle three and downing a bottle of rubbing alcohol, drop the basket and head out for a Tom Collins. Because, let's face it: After your innocent little shopping trip, ol' Tom might be the only man in your life right now.

COCKTAIL: *Tom Collins*

2 oz. gin
Liberal splash of homemade sour
mix *(see "Cheat Sheet")*
Liberal splash of club soda
Lemon slice

Mix ingredients together over ice in a collins

glass. Garnish with a lemon slice.

TIP JAR: Gin not your thing? You can easily
substitute vodka for a Vodka Collins.

CRISIS:

Okay, it's understandable—we *all* have those days when we haven't gotten around to doing laundry for a while and are forced to raid the dregs of the underwear drawer (read: where your stretched-out and faded panties with flowers and polka dots all over them go to die), and thanks to the ten-minute underwear search, you don't have time to shave your legs before going out. But when those two situations align on a Friday night and you find yourself about to leave the bar and hook up with a hot guy, nothing says "abstinence" better than granny panties and hairy legs. The only surefire way to stop worrying about what lies beneath your cute outfit and get it on with your handsome new prospect? March up to the bar and do two shots of tequila in quick succession.

COCKTAIL: Tequila Shot

> 2 oz. premium tequila *(think top shelf—you want to feel the effects without having a raging hangover the next day; shoot the cheap stuff and you'll be tasting it for weeks!)*

Pour an ounce into the shot glass and drink, sans lime or salt. (We call these two things "training wheels," which you don't need, right?—they're for amateurs!) Repeat as needed.

BONUS: Tequila, made from the agave plant, is the only liquor on the market that is actually a stimulant rather than a depressant—the last thing you want is to get sleepy mid-hookup. Also, of all the liquors, tequila is the lowest in carbs!

TIP JAR:
How to Prepare for
an Unexpected Hookup

....

1. Always have on hand (or in purse) the following: mint gum or strong breath mints (Tic Tacs usually don't do the trick), a spare contacts case (if you wear them), a condom (erring on the side of both fun and caution), and good lip gloss.

2. Even if you think there's no way in hell you're going to get action, it's always a good idea to shave your legs (and bikini line!) before hitting the town.

3. Ditto for wearing a decent bra and undies (bonus points if they're a matching set)—the stretched, faded, heart-speckled briefs aren't going to cut it on a Saturday night!

4. Try to arrange your apartment or house into semidecent order before you leave for the night—it's always better to bring the guy back to your place (thus avoiding any sort of walk of shame), and it's kind of embarrassing if he has to wade through your dirty laundry in order to get to the bed.

CRISIS:

In adult life the "walk of shame" takes on whole new dimensions, because now that we're not traipsing across a campus, it involves not only *walking*, but things like public transportation. And as much as you might want to pretend that teetering out of your guy's apartment at 8:00 a.m. on a sunny Saturday morning with bags (and mascara) under your eyes, wearing your outfit from the night before—stilettos and a miniskirt—while other people are walking with their babies and dogs is totally acceptable, well, let's just say a Morning-After Mimosa might make you see things a little more clearly!

COCKTAIL: *Morning-After Mimosa*

> 4 oz. champagne
> Splash of orange juice
> Orange slice or lemon twist

Combine in a champagne glass. Garnish with

an orange slice or lemon twist.

TIP JAR:
Hangover Cures

At Night:

- As soon as you get home, before you go to bed, guzzle as much water as humanly possible. (Make sure you avoid club soda or other fizzy drinks. Carbonation will speed up the amount of alcohol going into your blood and worsen the effects of the booze.)

- Eat something, preferably toast or crackers, which will stabilize your blood sugar (ameliorating that horrible wobbly feeling) without upsetting your stomach.

- Some people believe that taking aspirin or Tylenol at night will somehow help relieve the next day's pain. Not so. Aspirin will upset your stomach and make a hangover that much more painful. Acetaminophen (Tylenol) is even worse—when it mixes with the booze in your blood, it can cause serious liver damage. And your liver's been through enough grief for one night, don't you think?

- Take a multivitamin. Alcohol has flushed away all the vitamins that naturally stimulate your body's defense systems, leaving you completely unprotected.

A vitamin helps by replenishing some of the vitamins you've expelled during the course of the evening.

- If you can handle the acidity without throwing up, drink some orange juice. Vitamin C is essential because it speeds up the metabolism of the alcohol by the liver.

- More water (but make sure to use the bathroom a few times before passing out to avoid any "accidents!").

IN THE MORNING:
- Drink more water. We find slurping directly from the tap is effective and soothing.

- Take Alka-Seltzer to cure a sick stomach.

- Drink a sports drink (for rehydration and electrolytes), and throughout the course of the day, drink green tea with lemon (for detoxing). But make sure it's decaffeinated.

- Avoid caffeine at all costs. While some people swear by a strong cup of coffee in the morning, it's important to remember that caffeine dehydrates. Alcohol is extremely dehydrating, and the reason why your head

is pounding is because you're dried out. Drinking coffee will only make this worse. It's also a diuretic and will further upset your stomach.

- Try to eat as many fruits and veggies as you can throughout the day. Grease, contrary to popular opinion, is only going to make you bloated and slow down the detox process.

- Remember, you've just had a mild overdose of a depressant drug. So if you're feeling hypersensitive and wildly anxious, that's normal. If necessary, call in sick, put on a Lifetime movie, and sleep it off.

- One of the quickest ways to cure a hangover is to make a banana milk shake, sweetened with honey. The banana calms the stomach and, with the help of the honey, builds up depleted blood sugar levels, while the milk soothes and rehydrates your system. If this is too much work, just eat the banana-the potassium will work wonders!

It's Heating Up . . .

Nothing is more excruciating than first-date jitters—except for maybe second- or third-date jitters, when you know you are really into a guy and are trying your hardest to maintain a good first impression. But trust us, nothing says "desperate" like trying too hard, so take a deep breath and relax over one of these delicious drinks.

CRISIS:

How to put this one delicately? You've been dating someone for a while. You really like him. But when you finally sleep together, it is the worst sex you've ever had. Okay, so maybe we didn't put it so delicately, but a delicate Vodka Oyster Shot—sophisticated and, with the aphrodisiac element of the oyster, satisfying— is the *only* way you're going to get back in the game, put the vibe out there, and find someone who can actually keep up with you in the sack!

COCKTAIL: *Vodka Oyster Shot*

> 1 ½ oz. premium vodka, extremely chilled
> Splash of hot sauce
> 1 freshly shucked oyster

Combine all ingredients in a large shot glass or rocks glass. Bottoms up (to make way for bottoms off when you meet your next conquest!).

CRISIS:

First dates are a crapshoot. Sometimes you luck out and it's love at first sight. More often than not, though, right from the get-go, it's beyond painful. So if you're on a date with a guy who can't carry on a conversation or you just can't stand, order the always long and strong Gin Gimlet right away. The pucker on your face from the limey tartness will give him the hint that he's a boring dolt and you're not interested. Here's hoping you finish that drink alone!

COCKTAIL: *Gin Gimlet*

> 3 oz. premium gin
> Splash of bottled lime juice
> Splash of fresh lime juice
> Lime wedge

Shake everything with ice and serve straight up in a chilled martini glass or on the rocks in a rocks glass. Garnish with—what else?—a lime.

CRISIS:

You've been dating the perfect gentleman for two
months now. He's well dressed, well read, and has
a solid job as, let's say, an attorney for a big law firm.
Then one night, after the delicious dinner he's made
you at his apartment, you start making out, things
starts to escalate, and you're about to have sex. He
says, "Hold on a minute, honey," and just as you're
imagining what kind of massage oils and scented
candles he is about to procure, he reaches under his
bed to pull out a whip, a blindfold, some rope,
and a pair of handcuffs. You somehow missed
the "bizarrely kinky and possible serial killer"
vibe and have gotten yourself involved in a bad
(and potentially hazardous) situation. You
need a Kamikaze (literal translation: suicide
mission) shot. Enough said!

COCKTAIL: *Kamikaze Shot*

>1 ½ oz. premium vodka
>½ oz. triple sec
>Splash of lime juice

Shake all ingredients vigorously in a shaker with ice and pour into a shot glass. Suspend disbelief and drink! If a huge, strap-on dildo makes an appearance, triple the recipe!

CRISIS:

You met a guy online who claimed to be thirty-one, six foot three, and an extremely successful financial analyst. When you finally meet in person, however, he turns out to be in his late fifties, barely five six, and a school bus driver. A "perfect" Manhattan is what this moment calls for. Since you're now dating an old man, you need a grown-up cocktail. Plus, the cherry in the Manhattan is rich in antioxidants, which slow down the aging process. He may be an old fart, but cheer up—at least you'll stay forever young!

COCKTAIL: *"Perfect" Manhattan*

> 2 oz. bourbon
> $1/2$ oz. sweet vermouth
> Splash of maraschino cherry juice
> 1 plump maraschino cherry

In a shaker, pour bourbon, vermouth, and cherry juice over ice and stir. Strain into a martini glass and garnish with the cherry. Drink until you have "Manhattan goggles," which are a lot like "beer goggles," except they work even better!

TIP JAR: "Drunken cherries," which are the perfect accoutrement for a perfect Manhattan, are easy to make. Take fresh cherries and soak them in a jar with your favorite bourbon. Within hours, you'll have some pretty intoxicating fruit.

CRISIS:

Your relatively new and amazing almost-boyfriend just cooked you a huge gourmet Mexican meal. Afterward you're sitting on his couch watching *Grey's Anatomy* (we told you he's amazing!) when you shift to snuggle closer to him, and suddenly you expel something quite unladylike. Luckily, the TV volume is loud, so you do NOT acknowledge it. It just

didn't happen, because potential girlfriends don't pass gas. After an acceptable amount of time has elapsed (and the smell has dissipated under your rear end), casually excuse yourself, go to the kitchen, and down a Bitters and Club Soda (vodka optional, depending on the level of your mortification). Short of mainlining Maalox, this mixture is the next-best medicine and will instantaneously work wonders on settling that troublesome gut of yours.

COCKTAIL: Bitters and Club Soda

> 5 oz. club soda
> Liberal splash of bitters

Combine over ice and drink. Please burp before returning to the couch.

CRISIS:

You just found out your new boyfriend used to date a model. As in *Sports Illustrated* swimsuit issue, runway, face-of-Chanel model. He promises you that you're hotter, cooler, and smarter than she ever could be (not that you'd ever betray an iota of insecurity beyond asking a couple of "casual" questions about her), but you're still feeling a little bit, um, freaked out about the whole situation. What normal girl wouldn't? This calls for a Sunshine Cocktail made with diet soda. It's sweet and sunny (exactly how you should act every time her name is mentioned), plus you'll feel better with something on the low-calorie side since you've come across her bikini-clad, amazingly toned body in a magazine more than once!

COCKTAIL: *Sunshine Cocktail*

> 1 ½ oz. raspberry- or strawberry-
> flavored vodka
> 2 oz. diet fruit soda *(we like Fanta
> no-calorie grapefruit soda, but you can
> substitute any number of sodas, such as
> Sprite Zero or flavored seltzer)*
> Splash of orange juice
> Lemon or lime wedge

Pour the vodka and diet soda into a highball glass filled with ice and top with orange juice. Garnish with a lemon or lime wedge.

TIP JAR:
How to Get What You Want
in Any Situation

No, we're not taking on Tony Robbins—we just know what works, especially after spending five years behind a bar watching people! Whether it's a free drink, a new job, a million bucks, or the guy of your dreams, if you integrate the following simple things into your life, we promise you can (eventually) get everything your heart desires.

- Be Positive: You know the idea that by putting (forcing, if necessary) a smile on your face, you automatically start to feel better? That may be true, but trust us, while a big smile is an *excellent* first step in a positive outlook, you really need to *feel* it. Work out, stop talking smack about your coworker (in fact, get rid of whatever negativity you can from your life), or do whatever else it takes to get that inner glow (downing a bottle of Cabernet doesn't count). People will definitely notice.

- **Be Polite:** Nothing is more off-putting (or memorable) than someone who isn't at least nominally courteous. Your mom taught you how to say "please" and "thank you" for a reason.

- **Be Confident:** Even if you're quaking on the inside, appearing calm, cool, and collected—and confident—will get you infinitely further than kissing butt or crying over spilled milk (or vodka).

- **Surround Yourself with the Type of People Who Exhibit Qualities You'd Like to Have:** A recovering crackhead wouldn't (normally) keep living in the crack house, would she? Being around positive, supportive people will help to keep you on track.

CRISIS:

You decide it's time to introduce your new-ish boyfriend to your group of girlfriends. You and your guy meet up with your pals over drinks at your favorite girls-night-out hangout, and the worst-case scenario unfolds: There were more awkward exchanges than you care to count, and before you even get home, your phone is blowing up with texts about how he "isn't the one for you." First order of business: Dump his ass. Girlfriends know best, and, anyway, they're probably only confirming what your instinct was telling you already. Then immediately call the gals and reconvene over a round of Zen Tea Cocktails—on you, of course.

COCKTAIL: *Zen Tea Cocktail*

> 2 oz. premium vodka
> 3 oz. iced brewed green tea *(add sugar/sweetener and lemon while it's still piping hot for a deliciously smooth mix and then cool)*
> Chopped fresh ginger

Mix all ingredients with ice in a shaker and serve straight up in a chilled martini glass.

BONUS: Brewed tea is king in terms of health benefits—you can't beat the antioxidants therein, so however you can incorporate it into your routine, with alcohol or not, do it! Plus, it will give you the energy to find a new boyfriend.

You're on Fire!

You've finally earned the coveted moniker of "significant other," but that doesn't mean there aren't going to be bumps in the road. Sometimes maintaining a relationship can be more work than landing a guy in the first place. But think (and drink!) positively. Cheers to the good times and the bad!

CRISIS:

You cheated on your boyfriend and are paranoid he might find out. Relax, he doesn't know. (Unless it was with his hot best friend, whom you've been flirting with for the last two years, in which case, bravo, but you're totally busted.) Have your sister or best friend over to share a bottle of Pinot Noir. Red wine tends to calm even the jumpiest of nerves. If the weather is warm, you can make delicious sangria and achieve the same effect!

COCKTAIL: *Red Sangria*

A bottle of red wine
(sangria is a refreshing drink that doesn't require an expensive wine; we recommend a reasonably priced Spanish wine)
Chopped or sliced orange, lemon, and apple
1 Tbsp. sugar
3 generous splashes each of rum, triple sec, and and brandy
1 long splash of orange juice

Pour the wine into a pitcher filled halfway with ice, add the sugar, and stir until it is dissolved. In a separate bowl, pour the three liquors over the chopped fruit and stir, allowing the fruit to absorb the liquor. Add the drunken fruit to the wine mixture, then add orange juice. Stir together and serve. (You can allow the fruit to marinate in the liquor overnight to get the maximum amount of flavor. However, if you don't have the time, you can combine and serve immediately.)

P.S. If it was his hot buddy, all the sangria in Spain isn't going to get you out of this one!

BONUS: One glass of sangria has about 200 calories less than a margarita!

CRISIS:

You have been dating the perfect guy—at least on paper—for more than three years. While all your friends have been busy tying the knot with their beaus, you're still not convinced your man is The One. What you really need is a shot of truth serum to get you to reveal your innermost doubts, but if that's not available, substitute an Italian Mojito. Sweet cocktails like these are the next-best thing (alcohol sure has a way of bringing out our true feelings— bittersweet though they may be).

COCKTAIL: *Italian Mojito*

> 1 ½ oz. rum
> Freshly squeezed lime juice
> Dash of simple syrup
> Torn basil leaves
> Torn mint leaves
> Splash of Prosecco

Muddle the mint and basil in a shaker and top with ice, rum, lime juice, and simple syrup. Shake vigorously. Pour into a highball glass and top with Prosecco.

TIP JAR:
Wine 101

Red? White? Rosé? Sparkling wine? Dessert wine? Deciphering a wine menu can feel like reading Sanskrit text. When you're charged with ordering wine at the dinner table, don't panic! Choosing the perfect wine can be a painless process if you follow these easy guidelines.

- **First things first**: Find out what types of dishes people are ordering. If it's a big group, it's usually a good idea to get a bottle of white and a bottle of red to accommodate everyone's preferences. Easy rule of thumb: Red wine pairs well with red meats (beef, lamb, etc.), and white wine pairs well with white meats (poultry and fish). Why? Because if you're going to be eating something delicate and subtle, a strong wine could overwhelm the food. In the same vein, a hearty meal will often go best with a heavier wine. Wines that are more acidic are good with richer foods because they aid in digestion. For example, drinking a more acidic red wine with your lamb ragout will actually help you digest the calorific entrée.

- Another part of conventional wine wisdom says that beginning with lighter wines and progressing to heavier wines over the course of the meal is the way to go. You never want to start off with a heavy Cabernet and then move on to a light Pinot Noir because the complex earthiness of the Cabernet will overpower the subtle fruit of the Pinot Noir.

- Taste and preference are even more important than traditional pairings. Above all, our number one rule is: Drink what you like. We happen to love red wine and drink it with everything from salads to shrimp to steak.

- Don't forget: Even the most knowledgeable wine connoisseurs ask for help! Enlist your server, bartender, or sommelier for help with a recommendation in your taste (and price) range.

CRISIS:

You're madly in love with your boyfriend—
who happens to be sweet, smart, and a Greek
god doppelganger to boot. Everything has gone
swimmingly since you started dating. The only
problem? He has yet to say "I love you," and
you've been dating for over a year! You need
to make him (and yourself) a tall glass of Love
Potion No. 9. Basil is part of the mint family
and long believed to be a romance-inducing
herb—in present-day Italy, it is still a symbol
of love. If this concoction doesn't turn him
into a romantic, he's a cold fish and you need
to throw him back!

COCKTAIL: *Love Potion No. 9*

> 1½ oz. raspberry- or strawberry-
> flavored vodka
> 1/3 cup blueberries
> 1/3 cup strawberries
> Several fresh basil leaves

Muddle the berries and basil in a rocks glass
(but reserve one basil leaf for garnish) and stir
in vodka. Add ice and garnish with a basil leaf.

CRISIS:

One day you surprise your boyfriend by dropping by his office with a homemade picnic lunch. But the surprise is on you when you meet his new assistant for the first time. Her name is Helen, so you naturally assumed she was an over-the-hill grandma-type, but she turns out to be leggy (how unprofessional to be wearing a miniskirt in the office!) and drop-dead gorgeous. Apparently, your man never got the memo that said his assistants had to be over the age of seventy. In order to get over it, make him treat you to a Metropolitan (you're way too cool for a Cosmopolitan—his tacky assistant probably drinks those), not to mention an expensive dinner.

COCKTAIL: *Metropolitan*

2 oz. currant-flavored vodka
2 oz. cranberry juice
1 oz. fresh lime juice
Wedge of lime

Shake all ingredients with ice and serve straight up or on the rocks. Garnish with a lime wedge. Take a big gulp and swallow your insecurity.

CRISIS:

You and your boyfriend are utterly enamored with each other. You're spending almost every night together (your toothbrush is firmly in place next to his at his apartment, and he even lets you keep a box of tampons in his medicine closet). But there's trouble in paradise: He snores like a lawn mower, and you can barely sleep at night. Instead of suffocating him with a pillow or making him sleep on the couch (because when he's not sawing logs, you do love to snuggle!), why not make yourself a Rusty Nail before bed? After one of these, we guarantee you'll sleep through anything.

COCKTAIL: *Rusty Nail*

2 oz. whisky *(typically a high-quality blended Scotch such as Dewar's or Johnnie Walker works best in this scenario)*
2 oz. Drambuie

Combine and serve in a Scotch glass with an ice cube. Garnish with a pair of earplugs.

CRISIS:

You've reached the stage in your relationship where the lovey-doveyness is over and you're bickering . . . all the time. The couple that sips together stays together, so if you want to get over the hump, whip up a couple of Blue Hawaiians to take you right back to the honeymoon phase and remind you both why you fell in love in the first place.

COCKTAIL: *Blue Hawaiian*

> 1 oz. light rum *(you can also use coconut rum for an added tropical boost)*
> 2 oz. pineapple juice
> 1 oz. blue curaçao
> 1 cherry

Combine all ingredients with ice and shake vigorously. Serve on the rocks or up in a martini glass. Garnish with a cherry.

Tying the Knot

It's supposed to be the happiest day of your life, but greedy caterers (five hundred dollars a head?!), fussy florists, and controlling wedding planners are acting like a giant joy vacuum—sucking up all of the pre-wedding bliss and replacing it with anxiety and stress. The photographer has you on speed dial, the band raised its price by another thousand dollars at the last minute, and your dream venue just called to tell you they're closing for renovations. For these crises, a simple glass of sparkling white wine just isn't going to cut it!

CRISIS:

You called off your engagement. The last thing you want right now is a glass of champagne, since you're probably not exactly in the mood to celebrate (or then again, maybe you are)!

Ditch the bubbly for a Mint Julep. Mint has known healing qualities, including the ability to relax your muscles. You're no longer "tying the knot," and your neck muscles shouldn't be either!

Cocktail: Mint Julep

1 ½ oz. bourbon
Handful of torn mint leaves
Simple syrup
Club soda
Sprig of mint

Muddle the mint in a highball glass, fill glass with ice over the muddled mint, add bourbon and simple syrup, and stir. Top with a splash of club soda, garnish with a sprig of mint, and serve with several deep breaths!

CRISIS:

You've been dating your boyfriend for seven and a half years, and he's never broached the subject of marriage. You've tried to be subtle—subscribing to *Modern Bride,* cutting out pictures of a certain six-pronged, brilliant-cut diamond ring from the Tiffany's catalog and leaving them on his pillow—but he's just not getting the hint. You need a Champagne Cocktail, an elegant drink that will provide just enough liquid bravery so you can sit him down and demand to know his intentions, since nothing screams "I want to get engaged, you dolt!" like champagne mixed with something bitter. You're a smart, beautiful, strong woman, and you shouldn't have to wait around for another seven and a half years for this guy to get his act together!

Cocktail Therapy

COCKTAIL: *Champagne Cocktail*

> 4 oz. chilled champagne
> 1 sugar cube
> 2 dashes of bitters
> Lemon peel

Place the sugar cube in the bottom of a champagne flute and sprinkle it with two dashes of bitters. Top with champagne and garnish with a twist of lemon.

CRISIS:

You've finally found him—The One, your soul
mate. When he drops to one knee, your heart
starts racing. This is exactly how you've always
dreamed it would be—your fantasy proposal
is unfolding right before your very eyes. Every
nerve in your body is flooded with anticipation
as he slowly opens the tiny black velvet box
and reveals . . . a yellow-gold band with a
round diamond framed by pink baguettes—
hardly the platinum, Harry Winston, cushion-
cut solitaire you'd been hoping for. Love
the guy, hate the ring. When you go out to
dinner to celebrate, you need to order Liquid
Diamonds—if you can't wear your dream
bling, you might as well drink it!

COCKTAIL: *Liquid Diamonds*

    2 oz. premium gin
    1 oz. fresh lime juice
    1 oz. white cranberry juice
    Crushed ice

Combine all ingredients in a shaker and shake out all of your disappointment. Pour into a rocks glass over crushed ice. Sip while devising exactly how you're going to break the news to him that his taste in jewelry pales in comparison to his taste in women!

CRISIS:

Always the bridesmaid, never the bride. You open your closet and see a ghastly rainbow of taffeta gowns and pistachio- and tangerine-dyed satin pumps. You've spent your life's savings on engagement gifts, shower favors, and bachelorette parties. You've caught the bouquet several times, but you have yet to catch Mr. Right. Take advantage of the open bar during the cocktail hour of the next wedding you're a part of by drinking copious amounts of Vodka-Soda-Splash-of-Cran. This classic drink projects that you are a carefree, sophisticated woman, and the pastel color will complement your poofy, lavender bridesmaid's dress!

COCKTAIL:
Vodka-Soda-Splash-of-Cran

1 1/2 oz. vodka
3 oz. soda water
Splash of cranberry juice
Lime wedge

Fill a highball glass with ice and add vodka
and soda. Top with cranberry juice and garnish
with a wedge of lime. Give the cute bartender
your card. . . . Hey, you never know!

TIP JAR:
Basic Bar Etiquette

"The customer is always right" does not apply in a bar where alcohol is being served. Follow these simple rules, though, and you *will* always be right.

- Don't order a drink unless you have your money (or credit card) at the ready.

- Do not scream "Yo," "Hey, honey," and so forth, at the bartender. You will only wait longer.

- Have your order ready by the time the bartender gets to you.

- If a bartender takes care of you, take care of her. If you stiff a bartender out of a tip, trust us, she will remember you.

- Just because you like James Taylor doesn't mean everyone else does. Is it necessary to pump five bucks in the jukebox and play two *whole* James Taylor albums? The only time anyone wants to hear "Fire and Rain" is on a rainy Tuesday afternoon, after a sentimental run-in with an ex, *not* at prime drinking times.

- Would you walk into Banana Republic and expect a free pair of pants, just because you've shopped there in the past? The answer is no. So don't expect free drinks and buybacks. The bartender is under *no* obligation to give away alcohol. Ever.

- If a bartender *does* buy you a drink, you should (a) make sure you tip generously and (b) not expect another freebie every time you come back.

- If it's not cool for nineteen-year-olds to "bar neck," why would it be any better if you're over forty? PDA is gross. Don't do it.

CRISIS:

You are a meticulous bride-to-be whose attention to detail borders on compulsive. You have spreadsheets on your computer particularizing everything from the band's repertoire (in the order you'd like the songs performed) to which flowers are in season on your big day to an alphabetical listing of potential hors d'oeuvres. Although you promised yourself that you wouldn't become a Bridezilla, if the caterer can't procure Osetra caviar to top the potato puffs for the cocktail hour, you just might have a mental breakdown. You're driving everyone around you to drink, and you need a drink yourself. So take a deep breath and make yourself a Blueberry Cooler. Blueberries help protect the brain from oxidative stress, and researchers have found that blueberries significantly improve both learning capacity and motor skills—so you'll be back to a calmer version of your psycho, obsessive-compulsive self in no time!

COCKTAIL: Blueberry Cooler

1 ½ oz. vanilla vodka
⅓ cup blueberries *(plus extra for garnish)*
1 scoop of vanilla ice cream or frozen yogurt
1 Tbsp. honey
Handful of ice

Combine all ingredients in a blender and blend until smooth. Pour into a tall glass and sprinkle a few blueberries on top. Drink while sitting in the yoga Modra position.

CRISIS:

After months of tireless planning, the big day has finally arrived. But instead of feeling excited and joyful, you feel, well, kind of like packing a bag and leaving the country. Don't worry, it's perfectly normal to feel panicked on your wedding day. The perfect cure is a kir. The champagne will hopefully put you in more of a celebratory mood, and raspberries are very high in magnesium, which should help set you straight. (Studies have shown that an inadequate intake of magnesium can actually cause anxiety disorders.) So grab your bridesmaids and a bottle of crème de cassis and fix yourself a Cold-Feet Kir Royale!

COCKTAIL: *Cold-Feet Kir Royale*

> 3 oz. chilled champagne
> 1 oz. crème de cassis
> 1 oz. muddled raspberries

Spoon muddled raspberries into a champagne flute and top with champagne. Slowly stream in crème de cassis. Give your maid of honor your car keys—you're not going anywhere!

Till Death Do You Part

The trials and tribulations of lifelong commitment are starting to weigh you down like the proverbial ol' ball and chain. Not to worry—we have the perfect remedies for all marriage-related crises, for better or for worse!

CRISIS:

It's that time of the month, but instead of getting your period, you feel wildly nauseous. You're hoping your "error-proof" pregnancy test has made a *large* error when the little (+) sign shows up on the screen. This can't be happening. You just got married and you're already pregnant. OOPS! This situation calls for a Shirley Temple, since you'll be skipping the hard stuff for the next nine months or so. Plus, the ginger ale is a proven remedy to calm your stomach and relieve your morning sickness, and the cherries in the Shirley Temple are high in potassium and low in sodium, which will control water retention, which often results in the loss of excess water weight. Now that you'll be gaining baby weight, you need all the help you can get!

COCKTAIL: *Shirley Temple*

    4 oz. ginger ale
    Splash of grenadine
    Several maraschino cherries

Combine all ingredients in a highball glass
over ice.

CRISIS:

You're out to dinner with your girls, and the hot guy sitting at the neighboring table is totally checking you out. As you return his intense gaze, you suddenly remember that you're married and are allowed to be with only one man for the rest of your entire life! Panic starts to set in. Since you can no longer enjoy variety in your love life, we suggest subscribing to a wine club where you can sample new varietals every month.

Cocktail: *Wine Club*

There are lots of wine clubs out there—just do a quick Google search and you'll get a ton of results. We like wine.com: Each month they'll send you a bottle of white and a bottle of red from varying regions. You never have to drink the same wine twice. Go ahead and be a wine slut while still being a faithful wife!

CRISIS:

When you and your husband were dating, you had hot sex—sometimes up to four times a day. Now, with your busy schedules, kids, and crazy careers, you're lucky if you have sex once a week, and then it's always the boring missionary position. You need to spice up your sex life. Tonight, send the kids to your mom's, and when your husband gets home from work, meet him at the door with an Extra Hot and Dirty Martini. You get bonus points if you serve it *Pretty Woman*-style—wearing his favorite tie, stilettos . . . and nothing else!

COCKTAIL:
Extra Hot and Dirty Martini

2 oz. pepper-flavored vodka
Quick dash of dry vermouth
Liberal splash of olive juice
3 olives

Combine all ingredients (except garnish) in a shaker over ice and shake out your sexual frustration! Strain into a chilled martini glass and skewer three olives with a cocktail straw. When he comes through the door, suggestively suck one of the olives off the straw, then balance the straw on top of the cocktail glass!

CRISIS:

You look around and find that you and your friends went from a wild flock of social butterflies to a group of tired, overworked moms. How did this happen? To bring back some of the magic from the good old days, invite all of your girlfriends (and their kids) over for a playdate—juice for the kids, Momtinis for the moms. Remember, it's perfectly fine to balance your independent, social side with being a mother. You work hard, and you deserve some quality time with your girls over some delicious libations!

COCKTAIL: *Momtini*

1 ½ oz. peach-flavored vodka
1 oz. peach schnapps
Splash of freshly squeezed lime juice
Tiny splash of orange juice *(for color)*

Combine all ingredients in a shaker over ice.
Strain into a cocktail glass. If you feel like
having more than one, call a sitter!

CRISIS:

You are the first one in your group of tight-knit friends to get married. While you are shopping at Home Depot for a dish-drying rack with your husband, your friends are having brunch at a hot new restaurant without you, no doubt dishing about all the men they met out the night before while you were having a mellow dinner with your in-laws. Since you already have a ball and chain tethered to your ankle, you might as well enjoy the liquid version!

COCKTAIL: Ball and Chain

(A variation of the Rusty Nail—not for the faint of heart!)

> 2 oz. premium Scotch
> ½ oz. Drambuie
> Juice of half a lime *(to lighten things up a bit!)*
> Twist of lemon

Pour Scotch over ice in a rocks glass, float Drambuie on top, squeeze in lime juice, and garnish with a twist. Then, seriously, skip Home Depot and meet your friends. Remember: You're married, you're not dead!

Kicked to the Curb

A bad breakup can feel roughly akin to going through open-heart surgery fully conscious. Thankfully, we have something better than anesthesia: creative cocktails that will numb the pain and get you back in the game in a flash!

CRISIS:

You just got dumped by your long-term boyfriend out of the blue. Apparently, he wasn't seeing the relationship through the same rose-colored glasses that you'd been sporting. You need something strong that only a real woman can handle to remind yourself that you're a tough cookie who deserves someone who appreciates her: Whiskey on the rocks. Immediately. But only one. More than that and you might just fall victim to beer (or whiskey) tears, a definite setback.

COCKTAIL: *Whiskey on the Rocks*

> 2 oz. whiskey
> Ice

Fill a rocks glass with ice and then add whiskey. Serve with a tissue.

TIP JAR:
Whiskey Primer

"Whiskey" or "whisky" refers to a wide range of liquor made from grains and aged in oak casks. Most people don't know the difference between Scotch and bourbon, so we're here to shed some light on the subject. (Hey, they don't call us the "Whisky Chicks" for nothing!)

- **Whiskey vs. Whisky (when to use the "e")**: All whisky made in Scotland is spelled with the "y" only, no "e." All whiskey produced in Ireland and Canada takes the "e." Most American whiskies take the "ey" spelling as well, except for Maker's Mark, which opts for the no-"e" spelling as a shout-out to the owner's Scottish heritage.

- **Scotch**: Whisky from Scotland is called "Scotch." To earn the moniker of Scotch, whisky must be distilled (generally two times) and matured entirely within Scotland for a minimum of three years in oak casks.

- **Bourbon**: Bourbon is an American form of whiskey (actually, the only truly American spirit) made from at least 51 percent corn mixed with wheat and/or rye and malted barley. To be called "bourbon," the whiskey must be aged in new charred oak barrels for a minimum of two years. Although bourbon can be made anywhere in the United States, the spirit is largely associated with Kentucky. And trust us, there is no better way to enjoy a Mint Julep than at the Kentucky Derby!

- **Rye**: Think of rye as your grandfather's whiskey—not too popular with the young, hip city sets. Rye is a type of whiskey derived from a mash containing at least 51 percent rye. In the immortal words of Don McLean in "American Pie," rye is a drink for "them good ol' boys." It almost completely disappeared after Prohibition, and today very few distilleries continue to produce the spirit. Some popular Canadian brands still use a small amount of rye when making their whiskey.

CRISIS:

You want to call off a long-term relationship.
Mature woman that you are, you are resolved
to break up with your honey in person, talk it
out, and hopefully go home with a friendship
intact. This calls for a caffeinated vodka
mixed with some club soda and a slice of lime.
The vodka will provide some much needed
liquid courage, and the caffeine will give you
the strength to see it through.

COCKTAIL: *Caffeinated Club*

> 1 ½ oz. caffeinated vodka
> *(we prefer P.I.N.K., which is infused*
> *with caffeine and guarana)*
> Club soda
> Slice of lime

In a highball glass filled with ice, combine vodka and soda and garnish with the slice of lime.

NOTE: If he starts to cry, double the vodka dosage.

CRISIS:

Someone you really like just told you the feeling wasn't mutual. To soften the sting, you're going to need something stiff. While we rarely advocate Long Island Iced Teas, in this case, they're just what the doctor ordered.

COCKTAIL: Long Island Iced Tea

1/2 oz. vodka
1/2 oz. light rum
1/2 oz. gin
1/2 oz. tequila
1/2 oz. triple sec
Juice of half a lemon
Splash of Coke
Slice of lemon

Combine all five liquors and lemon juice in a highball glass over ice and stir. Top with Coke. Garnish with a slice of lemon. Drink half and then dump the rest over his head.

CRISIS:

You're on your way home from the gym, sweating like a pig and smelling like an old sock, when you see your ex-boyfriend walking toward you with his new girlfriend, who just happens to be a perfectly-put-together supermodel-type. You want to jump into a hole and hide, but it's too late—he's already spotted you. So you straighten your greasy ponytail, plaster a proud smile on your face, and say hello, trying to ignore the painful ache that is gathering in your heart. As soon as the excruciating moment is over and they are out of sight, head to the nearest purveyor of alcoholic beverages and get yourself a Snake Bite. You need something to dilute the venom that is coursing through your veins.

COCKTAIL: *Snake Bite*

1 oz. whiskey
1 oz. peppermint schnapps

Combine both ingredients over ice in a shaker
and strain into a shot glass.

CRISIS:

You just walked in on your boyfriend having sex with another woman . . . who happens to be one of your close friends! The betrayal is more than you can comprehend, and all you can do is head straight to another close friend's apartment to vent about what skanks your ex and ex-friend are and drink something to take the edge off. Such a tempestuous state of affairs calls for a Dark and Stormy.

COCKTAIL: *Dark and Stormy*

> 1½ oz. dark island rum
> 3 oz. ginger beer

Combine both ingredients in a highball glass over ice. Double the rum if she's your best friend. Triple the rum if she looks better naked than you do!

Work Woes

U nflattering lighting, ten hours of drudgery, an insane boss—work can often seem rather unappealing. But, alas, it is a necessary evil in a person's life. After all, if you don't work, how are you going to afford delicious cocktails?

CRISIS:

You're stuck in a fluorescent-lit cubicle doing data entry for an entire day. You contemplate killing the person who assigned you the task but are just too damn bored to do it. You need a liquid lunch! Since you still actually have to get some work done, an Espresso Martini will refresh you *and* give you that competitive edge.

COCKTAIL: *Espresso Martini*

> 1 shot espresso
> 1 oz. coffee-flavored liqueur
> 1 oz. vanilla vodka
> 1 oz. Irish cream liqueur
> Espresso beans

Brew one espresso and let cool. Combine all ingredients in a shaker over ice and shake. Serve straight up in a chilled martini glass (or disguised in a thermos if you choose to take it back to work!). Garnish with three espresso beans (they'll float on top).

CRISIS:

Your coworker just got the promotion that
you deserve, so why not meet that headhunter
who's been recruiting you for an after-work
Vodka Martini, straight up with an olive? A
martini shows that you're sophisticated and
can handle yourself well. In order to make sure
that you actually *can* handle yourself, don't
drink more than one, because martinis have a
way of sneaking up on you!

COCKTAIL: Vodka Martini

> 3 oz. premium vodka
> Dry vermouth
> 1 olive

Chill a martini glass and then pour a tiny splash of dry vermouth into it. Swirl it around to coat the glass, then shake out the excess so only the residue is left. Take your time shaking the vodka over ice, then pour straight up into the chilled martini glass coated with vermouth. Serve with one olive. (An even number of olives is bad luck, which is the last thing you need right now!)

TIP JAR:
Bar Terms

....

- **Up or Straight Up**: Term used to describe cocktails that are shaken over ice and then strained into a martini glass, thus ultimately served without ice.

- **Wet Martini**: A martini that is heavy on the dry vermouth.

- **Dry Martini**: A martini that has very little—or no—dry vermouth in it. A "bone dry martini" is the name people give to martinis made with just a whisper of dry vermouth.

- **In-and-Out Martini**: A martini prepared without dry vermouth, except for a small amount splashed into and then out of the requisite chilled martini glass.

- **Stirred**: A drink that is stirred instead of shaken will retain its clarity and be free of ice chips (see **Bruised**).

- **Shaken:** Instead of stirring, you can shake a drink. This works best with drinks that contain ingredients that are hard to mix, like cream, juices, and eggs. Shaking will also result in a colder beverage. No wonder James Bond prefers his martinis "shaken, not stirred."

- **Bruised:** By shaking alcohol with ice, you change the drink by creating little needles of ice and thus diluting it more than you would by stirring. The air bubbles and ice fragments created by shaking can make the martini cloudy or what's called "bruised."

- **Bitters:** A very concentrated flavoring agent made from roots, barks, herbs, and/or berries.

- **Chaser:** A mild drink, like soda or beer, taken after a hard liquor, especially a shot.

A lemon or lime wedge can also be used as a chaser.

- *Neat*: Term referring to liquor that is drunk alone—undiluted by ice, water, or mixers.

- *Training Wheels*: Term referring to the accoutrements needed to do a shot. For example, if someone orders a lemon drop, the sugar and lemon slice are the "training wheels."

- *Cut Off*: No more booze for you!

- *86'd*: Ditto. You don't have to go home, but you can't stay here! Also, if an item on the menu has been 86'd, that means the restaurant has run out of it. *Origin*: Chumley's, an awesome, cozy little former speakeasy at 86 Bedford in New York City's West Village (we love it there!), is where this term originated. During Prohibition, when the police were about to raid the speakeasy through its main entrance, the bartender would yell out "86," referring to the bar's street address. There was a side courtyard door through which patrons could make a speedy exit to avoid being arrested. Thank God those days are long gone!

- *On the House*: Music to your ears!

CRISIS:

It's Friday at 5:00 p.m. You're all packed
and ready to head to the Hamptons for the
weekend right from work when your boss
casually informs you that you'll be chained
to your desk all day Saturday and Sunday
dealing with a last-minute crisis. You have no
other options, so you passive-aggressively give
him a dirty look, then immediately recruit
as many of your friends as possible to meet
up someplace with an outdoor happy hour.
Promptly order a large margarita on the rocks.
Close your eyes and pretend you're happy;
when that doesn't work, take a large sip and
envision yourself at the beach.

COCKTAIL:
"I Wish I Were at the Beach" Margarita

2 oz. tequila
1 oz. orange-flavored liqueur
1 oz. fresh lime juice
Wedge of lime
Brightly colored cocktail umbrella
(optional)

Shake all ingredients in a shaker and serve on the rocks in a margarita glass. Garnish with the lime and a little cocktail umbrella, then serve with just a dash of self-pity!

CRISIS:

Your computer crashes, and all the data entry you've been doing for the last nine and a half hours is lost. The murder you contemplated earlier when the task was assigned becomes that much more feasible. Regroup by slipping some coffee liqueur into the mug on your desk to create an impromptu Coffee Cocktail.

COCKTAIL: Coffee Cocktail

An ounce of coffee-flavored liqueur will make any crappy office Sanka taste delicious. It'll be our little secret.

CRISIS:

All of the management at your company (including your immediate boss) has been out of town at a conference all week. You're taking advantage of the rare downtime by IMing your boyfriend. Although cybersex isn't normally your thing, you're bored, and the messages are starting to get really dirty. Suddenly, your boss pops his head into your office. Surprise! He came back a day early. In lieu of a cold shower, drink a slushy Key Lime Martini, you pervert!

COCKTAIL: *Key Lime Martini*

2 oz. vanilla vodka
1 oz. vanilla liqueur
1 oz. fresh lime juice
1 oz. pineapple juice
Wedge of lime

Shake all ingredients with ice and serve straight up in a chilled martini glass. Garnish with the lime wedge.

CRISIS:

Rumors have been swirling around the office about impending layoffs. You figure you're safe, given how indispensable you are, which is why you are so shocked when you get the pink slip—and no severance. This calls for a Dirty Gin Martini . . . or five. You can deal with finding a new job later. Right now you just need something that will kill the pain.

COCKTAIL: *Dirty Gin Martini*

> 3 oz. premium gin
> Dry vermouth
> Olive juice
> 3 olives

Fill a shaker with plenty of ice and a liberal splash of olive juice. Then add gin and a drop of dry vermouth and shake vigorously. Serve straight up in a chilled martini glass. . . . And don't forget to add three olives for the luck you need even more now!

CRISIS:

Your coworker constantly comes up behind you and, under the guise of "checking in" about your newest project, peers over your shoulder and blatantly reads all of your e-mails and listens in on all of your calls. The only possible antidote to this personal-space violator is a Kryptonite Cocktail. If this doesn't repel her, nothing short of rolling over her foot with your chair will!

COCKTAIL: *Kryptonite Cocktail*

> 2 oz. premium vodka
> Splash of olive juice
> 1 clove minced garlic
> Several small cocktail onions
> 1 olive

Combine ingredients and shake with ice. Serve straight up in a martini glass. Skewer an olive and several cocktail onions on a toothpick and balance the garnish atop the cocktail.

BONUS: Garlic is chock-full of benefits—it lowers blood pressure, helps prevent heart disease, and is an antioxidant, anti-inflammatory, and antibiotic. Plus, if it can ward off vampires, it should certainly work on a nosy coworker!

CRISIS:

From the moment you walk into work, you're craving something sweet, and vending machines stocked with Snickers bars, countless catered lunches complete with fudge brownies for dessert, boxes of holiday cookies, and your boss's Krispy Kreme addiction don't exactly help. Muster up all your willpower and resist the temptation to binge on something sugary. Instead, try to hold out for an after-work Sweetini. It will certainly satisfy your penchant for something sweet and decadent; plus, it will give you a nice little buzz, which you certainly can't get from a jelly doughnut!

COCKTAIL: *Sweetini*

2 oz. orange-flavored vodka
1 oz. orange juice
½ oz. fresh lime juice
Splash of champagne

Combine vodka and juices in a shaker over ice and then strain into a martini glass. Top with champagne.

CRISIS:

You've coasted along comfortably in your job for the last two years, arriving at the office sometime in the general vicinity of 9:30 a.m. and leaving at 6:00 p.m. on the dot every day. That is, until your new boss entered the picture. On her first day, when you were sailing out the door, she called you into her office and told you that you need to "check in" with her every day before leaving. Translation: She's a workaholic, and now you have to be too. Skulk back to your desk with your tail between your legs and exact the revenge you know best: Pour yourself a Grasshopper. It will help you ease into a new job search, and in the meantime, the minty flavor will give you fresh breath, all the better to kiss her butt with.

COCKTAIL: *Grasshopper*

> 1 oz. crème de menthe
> 1 oz. white crème de cacao
> *(use the clear version rather than the brown)*
> 3 oz. cream *(for a lighter variation, use regular or skim milk)*
> Peppermint patty

Combine ingredients in a shaker with ice.

Serve straight up in a chilled martini glass.

Garnish with a peppermint patty.

CRISIS:

You've been slaving over a deal at work for months, not to mention wining and dining the clients every night of the week. You're confident it's a "done deal" . . . until it suddenly implodes. In lieu of exploding, run out of the office and get yourself a Jäger Bomb—the energy drink will give you the added gumption to start a new project.

COCKTAIL: *Jäger Bomb*

> 1 oz. Jägermeister
> ½ can energy drink

Fill a shot glass with Jäger. Pour the energy drink into a collins glass, then drop in the shot glass. Shoot the whole thing. Garnish with a positive attitude.

CRISIS:

Due to recent belt-tightening and subsequent layoffs, your company is ridiculously understaffed, and although you feel lucky to still have your job (and are happy to demonstrate your can-do nature), you're actually doing the job of seven people . . . and it's catching up with you. The solution? Since you feel as stressed as a double agent, indulge immediately in a 007.

COCKTAIL: 007

2 oz. orange-flavored vodka
2 oz. orange juice
2 oz. lemon-lime-flavored soda
Orange slice

Combine ingredients with ice in a collins glass. Garnish with an orange slice.

CRISIS:

Months ago you scheduled a meeting with your
boss so you could negotiate a higher salary.
The day of the meeting finally comes around,
and you're just about to launch into your
prepared speech on exactly why he should show
you the money when suddenly the fire alarm
goes off. You're hoping it's just a drill, but
you can hear fire engines approaching in the
distance. After safely evacuating the building,
why not sneak into a bar and score yourself
a Flaming Dr Pepper? The high-proof,
flammable rum will give you the chutzpah
to march back into your boss's office and
continue right where you left off . . . once the
smoke clears, of course!

COCKTAIL: *Flaming Dr Pepper*

½ oz. amaretto
Splash of 151-proof rum
½ glass beer

Fill a shot glass three quarters of the way with amaretto. Float the rum on top. Fill a pint glass halfway with beer. Light the shot on fire, drop the shot into the beer, and chug.

TIP JAR:
Make sure the flame is extinguished before guzzling. Duh!

CRISIS:

You and a coworker are saddled with finishing a project by 9:00 a.m. the following day, even if it takes all night. The two of you are working fervently into the wee hours of the morning, and while your colleague gets his midnight lift from the dealer down the street, why not treat yourself to a shot of Liquid Cocaine? Hey, at least your vices are legal!

COCKTAIL: *Liquid Cocaine*

> ½ oz. 151-proof rum
> ½ oz. Goldschläger cinnamon schnapps
> ½ oz. Jägermeister

Combine all ingredients in a shaker over ice and stream into a shot glass. If you plan on actually getting some more work done, allow yourself only a single shot.

CRISIS:

One of your coworkers, who started at the same time as you, has been sleeping her way to the top. While you're stuck answering phones and copyediting interoffice memos, she just landed a corner office. Instead of sending a companywide e-mail outing her for being such a whore, take out your frustrations by enjoying a Redheaded Slut after work.

COCKTAIL: Redheaded Slut

> 1 oz. peach schnapps
> 1 oz. Jägermeister
> Splash of cranberry juice

Combine all ingredients in a shaker over ice. Pour into a shot glass and shoot!

CRISIS:

The new guy you've been crushing on at work for weeks casually mentions his boyfriend in passing, and then you're *really* crushed! Gaydar is a good skill to hone, but like everything else, sometimes it's faulty. This calls for a California Bay Breeze, a drink as sweet and fruity as your new work *friend*!

COCKTAIL: California Bay Breeze

> 2 oz. Malibu rum
> *(or any other coconut rum)*
> 2 oz. cranberry juice
> 2 oz. pineapple juice
> 1 cherry

Combine everything in a highball glass with ice. Garnish with a cherry.

CRISIS:

You've been working until four in the morning
for the last ten days, discovering new meanings
to the term "burnout." Since you consistently
get home right before sunrise, why not treat
yourself to a Tequila Sunrise? After all, you're
burning the candle at both ends, and you need
all the immune system support you can get.
The vitamin C in the orange juice will provide
you with tons of antioxidant protection so you
won't get sick, while the tequila will help make
your outlook just a little bit sunnier.

COCKTAIL: *Tequila Sunrise*

> 2 oz. tequila
> 4 oz. orange juice
> Splash of grenadine
> Orange slice

Mix tequila and orange juice in a highball glass over ice. Slowly stream in grenadine while slanting the glass. The grenadine should sink to the bottom and then rise to the top, creating a "sunrise." Garnish with an orange slice.

CRISIS:

You're messing around with your hot coworker after-hours in the copy room; you're only human, after all, and this work thing is getting to be a real drag. Things are just starting to heat up when the office secretary walks in and catches you in the act! You both need a Blow Job Shot immediately.

COCKTAIL: *Blow Job Shot*

½ oz. Irish cream liqueur
½ oz. amaretto
Whipped cream

Combine Irish cream and amaretto in a shot glass and top with a mound of whipped cream. Have your coworker put his hands behind his back, then pick up the shot glass with his mouth, tilt his head back, and drink. Now it's your turn.

 TIP JAR: You can use the extra whipped cream for whatever your dirty little hearts desire, but this time, so you both don't lose your jobs, please, GET A ROOM!

The Hole in Your Pocket

You just got home from your low-paying job to find that your monthly bills have arrived, and the amount owed is more than your yearly salary. The collection agencies have you on speed dial, and if your rent check bounces one more time, you'll have to move back in with your parents. Let's just hope you have a little charging power left on that credit card for a tasty drink to take the edge off.

CRISIS:

What to do when creditors call? Ignore your ringing phone and head to the market to grab a 40-ounce bottle of Colt 45. It's cheap as hell and will wipe out *all* of your thoughts—including your financial woes.

COCKTAIL: Colt 45

Self-explanatory. However, when purchasing, head as far away as humanly possible from your neighborhood. You're one step away from panhandling, and this just doesn't look good.

CRISIS:

You just started a new job and found out it's going to take six weeks for HR to process your paperwork before you can start getting paid. Six weeks of no pay calls for a six-pack of one of the cheapest and best beers out there. Say it with us: "PBR me ASAP!"

COCKTAIL: Pabst Blue Ribbon

Crack open a can and pair with salty peanuts (also dirt cheap) for optimum enjoyment.

TIP JAR:
All About Beer

People have been drinking beer for centuries for a reason! It's refreshing, cheap, and, unlike some cocktails, beer is available at just about every bar in the world. (Keep in mind: Ordering a Passion Fruit Bellini at a dive bar just might get you beat up!) All the different, delicious varieties of beer generally fall under two categories: lager or ale. Each differs in the type of yeast used to brew it and the temperature at which it's brewed.

There are four main types of lager:

- American pale lager usually contains more carbonation than the other types of beer. It tends to be light in color and body (e.g., Budweiser).

- Pilsner is also pale, but it tends to be more flavorful and more bitter than American-style pale lagers (e.g., Pilsner Urquell).

- *Light lager* has less calories! Light beer also has a slightly lower alcohol concentration than regular beer (e.g., Harp).

- *Dark lager* has a richer flavor, a very dark color, and a full-bodied taste (e.g., Beck's Dark).

There are also four main types of ale:

- *Pale ale* uses ale yeast and mostly pale malts to get its distinctive flavor (e.g., Bass, Sierra Nevada).

- *Brown ale* is usually red or copper in color and has a milder flavor than the other types of ale beer (e.g., Newcastle).

- *Porter* is dark and full-bodied, and has a chocolatey flavor (e.g., Anchor).

- *Stout* is the darkest type of beer, almost black in color. Stouts are thick and strong (e.g., Guinness).

CRISIS:

Rent was due three weeks ago, and the landlord's threatening to toss you out. Remember when you first moved in four years ago and your next-door neighbor borrowed a cup of sugar? It's payback time. A couple of ounces of her vodka is certainly a fair trade. Just add ice. It's free.

COCKTAIL: Vodka on the Rocks

Pour borrowed vodka over free ice from your freezer. Enjoy!

CRISIS:

Your credit card bill just arrived. You somehow managed to forget your "little" splurge at Forever 21, but the credit card company sure didn't. On your way back from returning the crap you'll probably never wear anyway, put that extra money to good use and get yourself a Bourbon Bee Sting. It's so decadent and sweet that you'll forget all about ridiculously high APR rates.

COCKTAIL: Bourbon Bee Sting

2 oz. bourbon
Splash of simple syrup
2 oz. pomegranate juice

Combine all ingredients and serve over ice.

CRISIS:

Your car breaks down, and your friendly mechanic tells you it's going to cost a cool grand to get it up and running again. Now that you're walking home from work, add to your normal bottle of water a packet of Crystal Light lemonade powder and a liberal splash of spiced island rum.

COCKTAIL: Tropical Lemonade

> 2 oz. spiced island rum
> 1 powder packet of Crystal Light
> Bottle of water *(chilled)*

Pour rum and Crystal Light into the water bottle, screw on the cap, and give it a good shake. Presto! You have an on-the-go Tropical Lemonade and a bonus: No DWI!

CRISIS:

Once again, you've been abusing your checking account's overdraft protection, and you're bouncing checks left and right. Now that you have hit rock bottom, borrow some cash from a friend and get yourself a Bottom Bouncer.

COCKTAIL: Bottom Bouncer

> 1½ oz. Irish cream liqueur
> 1½ oz. butterscotch schnapps
> 1 oz. amaretto

Shake ingredients with ice and strain into a martini glass. You can't exactly afford dinner right now, so eat whatever bar snacks are available—peanuts, pretzels, hard-boiled eggs . . . anything!

CRISIS:

You just bought your first home and are so excited! But bridge loans, closing costs, lawyer fees, and mortgage payments are slowly killing your buzz. Plus, who knew furniture could be so expensive? And the plumber just told you that the little leak under the kitchen sink is going to cost over a thousand dollars to fix due to water damage. Since this new purchase of yours is giving you a run for your money, why not indulge in a Money Pit?

COCKTAIL: *Money Pit*

1 ½ oz. premium gin
1 oz. orange juice
Dash of pastis
Dash of grenadine
Orange slice

Combine all ingredients (except orange slice)
in a shaker over ice. Shake and then strain
into a chilled cocktail glass. Garnish with the
orange slice.

CRISIS:

Your tooth has been killing you for weeks, and you finally go to the dentist to get it checked out. It turns out you have to have an emergency root canal . . . and you don't have dental insurance! Unless you want the tooth to rot and fall out, you'll have to pay thousands of dollars out of your own pocket to get it fixed. In addition to plenty of laughing gas and novocaine, we recommend an Orgasm. The drinkable kind. If your tooth is sore after the painful procedure, double (or triple!) the recipe for multiple orgasms.

COCKTAIL: Orgasm

¹/₂ oz. white crème de cacao

¹/₂ oz. amaretto

¹/₂ oz. triple sec

¹/₂ oz. vodka

¹/₂ oz. light cream or whole milk

Shake all ingredients with ice and strain into a chilled martini glass.

BONUS:

Research has proven that during orgasms (the real kind) humans can withstand normally intolerable levels of pain. We'd be remiss in not mentioning that!

CRISIS:

You went *waaaaaaay* over your minutes on your
cell phone plan yet again and ended up with a
$600 phone bill. You call the company crying,
but the bored representative can't do anything
to help you. And if you don't cough up the
dough within two weeks, your service will be
cut off. During rocky times like these, aim for
a cheap rendition of Jack Daniel's: the good ol'
standby Early Times—on the rocks, of course.

COCKTAIL: *Early Times on the Rocks*

3 oz. Early Times whiskey
Ice

Serve on the rocks in a rocks glass.

TIP JAR: When buying really cheap liquor, beware of the hangover—the reason it's so wonderfully *cheap* is because it hasn't been distilled as much as the more pricey stuff. That's why it's much less smooth, too. Also, while we're on the subject, in terms of hangovers, a general rule of thumb is the darker the liquor, the worse the hangover.

CRISIS:

Your close friend is in a financial crisis of her own, and you graciously lend her a significant amount of money. She's incredibly grateful, and you feel good . . . until she forgets about the loan. Six months later she's detailing her latest shopping binge on Madison Avenue while you seethe. It's the elephant in the room, so it calls for a big cocktail—namely, Jungle Juice. Normally a frat-party favorite, it's a strong drink that packs a punch and is guaranteed to give you the confidence to step up and ask for your money back.

COCKTAIL: *Jungle Juice*

    1 oz. whiskey
    1 oz. Southern Comfort
    1 oz. peach schnapps
    2 oz. orange juice
    2 oz. Hawaiian Punch
    Orange slice

Combine all ingredients and serve on the
rocks. Garnish with an orange slice.

CRISIS:

Preferring to spend your extra money on fun dinners and nights out with the girls, you're not normally a huge shopper. That is, until you happen by the most gorgeous fur-trimmed cashmere coat you've ever seen, which completely haunts you for days to come. The $3,000 price tag is entirely out of your league, though, and the only way to get the coat you covet off your mind is with a Mind Eraser.

COCKTAIL: *Mind Eraser*

> 1 oz. premium vodka
> 1 oz. coffee-flavored liqueur
> 3 oz. club soda *(tonic water also works for an extra zing)*
> Straw

Pour all three ingredients into a rocks glass and promptly suck down with a straw.

CRISIS:

You've just come back from a blissful honeymoon and could not be more in love with your new husband. After combining your bank accounts, you go out for a little afternoon shopping . . . and end up "accidentally" charging a couple grand on your shared credit card. You are anxiously awaiting the day when the bill arrives since you bought everything in town—including a one-way ticket to the doghouse. When it does arrive, head to your neighborhood bar and order yourself a Money Shot.

COCKTAIL: *Money Shot*

½ oz. melon liqueur
½ oz. white tequila
½ oz. Jägermeister
Splash of cranberry juice

Combine all ingredients in a shaker over ice and strain into a shot glass. Pay for it with cash—the last thing you need is another charge on your card!

CRISIS:

Your husband just filed for divorce, citing
the irreconcilable differences you both have
been ignoring for the last five years. Since
you'll soon be dividing the assets, you've got
money on your mind, so why not order a
Goldschläger? Goldschläger is a brand of
cinnamon schnapps with genuine 24-karat
gold-leaf flakes in it. The smell of cinnamon
is proven to actually boost brain activity, which
will come in handy when you have to prove in
a court of law that you are entitled to your fair
share of everything. And now that you have
to give up the sparkler on your left ring finger,
you might as well get your daily allowance of
bling in a cocktail.

COCKTAIL: Goldschläger Neat

2 oz. Goldschläger cinnamon schnapps

Pour into a snifter or rocks glass and sip while flipping through the Yellow Pages for a good attorney!

Little Annoyances

We've all been there. While en route to an important meeting, roadwork has gotten traffic backed up for miles and you could commit murder. Or you break a nail twenty minutes after an expensive manicure, and you feel the urge to cry hysterically. Throughout the day, any one of life's millions of mini-crises may be hurled in your direction . . . but the world isn't going to stop just because your crisp white shirt is now decorated with an overpriced soy latte from Starbucks. We've learned that life's teeny-tiny (in the grand scheme of things) bitter pills go down much easier with a spoonful of sugar-free liquid tranquility, and we are firm believers that when life hands you lemons, why not make a Lemon Drop?

CRISIS:

The dry cleaner shrunk your favorite pants—either that or you've put on a few pounds. (Face it: Neither option is all that appealing!) Why not dissolve your irritation in a Sugar-Free Mojito?

COCKTAIL: Sugar-Free Mojito

    1 oz. rum
    Juice of half a lime

Large handful of torn mint leaves
2 or 3 packets of Splenda
Crushed ice
Sprig of mint

Blend all ingredients in a blender until smooth. Garnish with a sprig of mint. Sip in between lunges, push-ups, and crunches!

TIP JAR: Like we said, a spoonful of sugar (or sweetener!) helps the medicine go down. In most cocktail recipes, sugar or "simple syrup" (i.e., sugar water) is added to smooth out the flavor of the alcohol. Splenda, Equal, or other sugar substitutes are perfect alternatives because they dissolve completely in the cocktail and sweeten without hurting your waistline. We're not saying you're fat! But it's amazing just how many calories are in our favorite drinks. Wherever we can cut some out, we make low-cal substitutions. Another way to trim some of the fat? Substitute club soda for calorie-filled tonics and juices.

TIP JAR:

Calories in the Bar

....

EARNING VS. BURNING

EARNING
(calories consumed per drink)

- Margarita: up to 500 calories
- Red or white wine: 90 calories
- Regular beer: up to 200 calories
- Light beer: 90 calories
- Shot of whiskey: 100 calories
- Vodka tonic: 240 calories
- Vodka soda: 100 calories

BURNING (calories burned per hour)

- Playing darts: 176 calories
- Playing pool: 167 calories
- Dancing: 317 calories
- Sitting at the bar: 60 calories
- Standing at the bar: 90 calories
- Making out: 100 calories
- Sex (just in case!): 140 calories

CRISIS:

You get takeout and don't realize until you get home that the restaurant gave you something completely different from what you ordered. You definitely don't feel like leaving the house again, so why not scrounge around for that lone Kiwi Strawberry Wine Cooler that's been sitting in the back of your fridge since you bought a pack for Aunt Matilda when she came to visit last spring? The sickeningly sweet fizz will distract you from the fact that you're not going to get that burger you've been craving and are stuck with a soggy grilled cheese.

COCKTAIL:
Kiwi Strawberry Wine Cooler
Available at your local liquor store!

CRISIS:

You got caught in the rain without an umbrella.
Your grandparents believed a little "cough
medicine"—euphemism for whiskey—kept the
sniffles at bay, and the same theory applies here.
When you finally get out
of those wet clothes,
curl up on your couch
with a soothing Hot
Toddy. The medicinal
quality of the
whiskey mingling
with honey will
help to warm you
up, melt away your
aggravation, and stave
off a raging cold to boot!

Cocktail Therapy

COCKTAIL: Hot Toddy

1 oz. bourbon
1 glass hot black tea
2 Tbsp. honey
Juice of half a lemon
Lemon slice studded with 2 cloves

Brew tea and dissolve honey in tea. Pour in
bourbon and lemon juice, then allow lemon slice
with cloves to float on top and scent the cocktail.

CRISIS:

Your flight is delayed indefinitely. Head straight to the ubiquitous airport bar and order a refreshing White Wine Spritzer. You don't know

how long you'll be stuck there, so you're better off imbibing something light that you can keep ordering. It will be that much easier to sleep (and ignore the loud breather sitting next to you) when you eventually make it on the plane.

COCKTAIL: *White Wine Spritzer*

> White wine *(we usually prefer Sauvignon Blanc or Pinot Grigio because each is crisp, fruit-forward, and not too dry)*
> Club soda
> Slice of lime

Pour wine into an ice-filled wineglass and top with club soda. Garnish with a lime. Once you're on board, add half an Ambien tablet as a second garnish. Lights out!

 TIP JAR: For a really impressive added touch when serving spritzers at home, zest a lemon, lime, and/or orange using a zester or grater. Put the pretty, colorful strands of zest into an ice cube tray, then fill with water. In a few hours you'll have fancy ice cubes to put in your spritzers. As the ice melts, the zest will add even more flavor and freshness to the cocktail.

Whether you're on a date or out with business colleagues, if you're drinking wine and want to impress, you need to have a working wine vocabulary.

* Fruity: Use this adjective when you can taste fruit flavors in the wine. Many white wines have a crisp, green-apple flavor because of the high malic acid content. Often in lighter bodied red wines you can taste strawberry, while other reds might be described as having strong hints of cherry and currant.

* Spicy: When a wine is peppery or cinnamony, call it "spicy." Rhônes are typically spicey reds.

* Buttery: More upscale white wines, particularly oak-aged Chardonnay from California, can sometimes taste like melted butter or toasted oak. "Buttery" can also be used to describe the texture of a glass of wine.

* Legs: When you swirl your wine around the glass, you will see little rivulets streaming down the sides of the glass, called "legs." They tell you how much

alcohol and sugar the wine contains. The higher the alcohol or sugar content, the slower the legs fall. A wine with "great legs" is usually made from ripe fruit, so it is very alcoholic and sugary. So when the new guy in your office shouts "nice legs" at a corporate dinner, don't be so quick to slap him!

* Seductive: A wine you just want to slurp down because it's so delicious can be called "seductive."

* Flabby: Use this adjective to describe wine that is "weak in the ass"—not very bold or flavorful.

* Body: This term refers to how the weight of a wine feels on your palate. The more alcohol a wine has, the fuller it will feel on your tongue. This is referred to as "body."

* Young: This can mean one of two things: a wine that has not yet matured fully, or a fresh, youthful, bright wine, which is meant to be drunk in its first few years.

* Finish: A "finish" describes the feeling and taste in your mouth after you swallow. A good wine has a nice, long finish.

CRISIS:

The impossibly high heel on your brand-new
shoe breaks right as you strut into a cocktail
party. Immediately grab a Passion Fruit Bellini
from a passing waiter. It will give you a much
needed boost of class as you limp your way
through the, er, "well-heeled" crowd.

COCKTAIL: Passion Fruit Bellini

> 2 oz. chilled passion fruit puree *(see "Cheat Sheet")*
> Chilled champagne
> Fresh raspberries *(strawberries are* très *gauche this season!)*

Spoon the puree into a champagne flute and top with champagne. The champagne bubbles should act as tiny stirrers and evenly distribute the puree; however, if the puree settles to the bottom, give the cocktail a gentle stir. Garnish with a raspberry.

CRISIS:

It's early Monday morning, and you've just arrived at work when your klutzy coworker bumps into you, spilling her steaming mochaccino all over your new winter white blazer. White Sangria is the perfect antidote for this calamity—you need something cold and stain-resistant!

COCKTAIL: *White Sangria*

   1 cup water
   ½ cup sugar
   4 cinnamon sticks
   Freshly grated nutmeg *(optional)*
   1 bottle of white wine
   (Spanish wine, such as Rioja, works
   best, but Sauvignon Blanc is fine
   as well; avoid an oaky California
   Chardonnay at all costs!)
   1 cup soda water
   1 cup apple juice
   2 sliced oranges
   2 apples *(cut into chunks)*
   A dozen sliced strawberries or whole
   cherries *(or both!)*

While soaking your blazer in cold water to
break up the coffee stain, heat the cup of water
with the half cup of sugar, cinnamon sticks, and
nutmeg. Simmer for 5 minutes, until sugar is

entirely dissolved. Cool to room temperature.
Remove the cinnamon sticks and add wine, soda
water, juice, and fruit to the sugar-spice mixture.
Chill and serve over ice. Garnish with an orange
slice.

CRISIS:

Your toilet is clogged. Call it crude, but we just can't
help ourselves: This situation calls for a Mudslide!

COCKTAIL: Mudslide

1 oz. vodka
1 oz. Irish cream liqueur
1 oz. coffee-flavored liqueur
Generous scoop of vanilla ice cream
Splash of milk
Handful of ice cubes
Chocolate bar

On your way to the hardware store to buy a plunger, swing by the grocery store and pick up vanilla ice cream, milk, and a chocolate bar, then run into the liquor store for the rest of the reinforcements. When you arrive at home, immediately take care of the toilet issue and then wash your hands vigorously with antibacterial soap. Next, in a blender, combine vodka, Irish creme liqueur, coffee-flavored liqueur, ice cream, milk, and a handful of ice cubes. Blend until smooth. Pour into a tall glass and garnish with shavings from the chocolate bar.

BONUS: Chocolate is full of bioactive compounds that are proven to lessen anxiety while promoting well-being—just what the doctor ordered after an afternoon spent plunging!

 TIP JAR: For perfect chocolate shavings, all you need is an ordinary vegetable peeler. Just run the peeler steadily across the chocolate bar lengthwise, applying equal pressure all the way down.

CRISIS:

You get locked out of your apartment in the middle of January. There's a foot of slushy snow on the ground, it's freezing, and none of your roommates are answering their phones. Trek to the nearest purveyor of alcoholic beverages and order a toasty Snuggler. Its peppermint sweetness will relax and soothe your nerves, while the hot chocolate will warm your bones.

COCKTAIL: *Snuggler*

1 oz. peppermint schnapps
1 cup steaming hot chocolate
Whipped cream

Prepare hot chocolate according to package directions and add peppermint schnapps. Top with whipped cream. Repeat until one of your roommates finally calls you back.

CRISIS:

You just finished thoroughly cleaning your apartment. The place is spotless . . . until you knock over your roommate's enormous, ugly houseplant, spilling soil and sending shards of pottery all over the floor. Don't cry over spilled dirt—especially when you have milk in the fridge for a frothy White Russian.

COCKTAIL: *White Russian*

> 2 oz. vodka
> 1 oz. coffee-flavored liqueur
> 2 oz. light cream or milk

In a shaker, combine vodka, coffee-flavored liqueur, and cream or milk over ice. Take out your frustration by shaking vigorously! Serve in a rocks glass over ice.

BONUS: Riboflavin in milk helps produce energy in the body's cells, and you're going to need all the energy you can get to clean up this mess!

CRISIS:

You're in your kickboxing class, and the guy working out on the bag next to you is sweating up a storm. Each time he swings, you're showered in his gross perspiration. In lieu of punching him in the face, procure a tall glass of Planter's Punch as soon as the class is over.

COCKTAIL: *Planter's Punch*

> 1 oz. light rum
> 1 oz. dark rum
> Liberal splash of pineapple juice
> Splash of orange juice
> Splash of grenadine
> Splash of 151-proof rum
> Thick slice of orange or pineapple

In a shaker over ice, combine all ingredients up to but not including the 151-proof rum. Shake angrily to vent all the disgust that built up during your workout. Pour into a rocks glass over ice, then splash the 151-proof rum on top as a floater. Garnish with an orange or pineapple slice.

CRISIS:

You're cruising home from work when the highway suddenly gets extremely bumpy. You realize, much to your horror, that you have a flat tire . . . and you don't have a spare. This minor tragedy calls for a Hitchhiker—after all, you won't be driving yourself home!

Cocktail Therapy

COCKTAIL: Hitchhiker

2 oz. raspberry-flavored vodka
1 oz. triple sec
Juice of half a lime
Splash of cranberry juice
Small handful of torn mint leaves
Twist of lemon or lime wedge

Muddle mint in the bottom of a shaker and then add remaining ingredients with ice. Shake and then strain into a chilled martini glass. Garnish with a twist of lemon or a lime wedge.

CRISIS:

You accidentally put your favorite cashmere sweater in the dryer, and now it looks like it's too small for Barbie! Since there's no way to stretch your sweater back to normal size, why not treat yourself to a Shrinking Violet cocktail?

COCKTAIL: *Shrinking Violet*

2 oz. vanilla-flavored vodka
1 oz. crème de cassis
Liberal splash of lime juice
Small handful of fresh raspberries
Lime wedge

Crush raspberries in the bottom of a shaker, then add all remaining ingredients with ice. Shake and then strain into a chilled martini glass. Garnish with a lime wedge.

CRISIS:

You're running late for work, and in your haste you slam your finger in the car door. The pain is throbbing harder and harder with each heartbeat. It's seven thirty in the morning and you're already having a bad day. You feel like banging your head against the wall, but instead, why not fantasize about the Harvey Wallbanger you'll enjoy when the long day is finally over?

COCKTAIL: Harvey Wallbanger

1 oz. vodka
2 oz. orange juice
1 oz. Galliano
Cherry

Combine vodka and orange juice over ice.
Float Galliano on top. Garnish with a cherry
(and extra ice for your injured finger!).

CRISIS:

Your adorable new puppy just peed like a
racehorse all over your (also new) living
room carpet. Nothing inspires patience and
puppy love like a Salty Dog, a drink that
will steel you for the cleanup process ahead.
The grapefruit juice is tart and tangy with an
underlying sweetness,
just like you
have to be
when training
your new pet!

Cocktail Therapy

COCKTAIL: *Salty Dog*

2 oz. premium vodka
5 oz. grapefruit juice
1 tsp. salt
Lime wedge

Mix everything in a shaker with ice and pour into a highball glass. Garnish with a wedge of lime. Extra points if you take the time to salt the rim!

 TIP JAR: Salty Dogs, margaritas, and other cocktails gain additional flair when you salt (or sugar, as the drink may require) the rim of the glass. While the glass is empty, take a lime wedge and run it around the rim—making it good and sticky. Pour about half a cup of kosher salt or sugar (turbinado sugar works best because the crystals are bigger) onto a small plate. Dip the rim of the glass in the sugar or salt. Voila!

CRISIS:

We've all been there. You spent months or even years growing your hair out, and now it's long and glossy, falling all the way down your back, just the way you like it. You need a trim, though, and advise your stylist to take as little off the bottom as possible. But, inexplicably, you've been left with a shoulder-skimming pageboy. Because you no longer have any hair on your head, you need some Hair of the Dog.

COCKTAIL: Hair of the Dog

Normally reserved for brunch the morning after a big night out (the usual suspects include Bloody Marys, mimosas, screwdrivers, etc.), this special appearance of the Hair of the Dog is "choose your own adventure" style. So pick whatever cocktail makes you feel pretty. Just don't drink too much or you might be tempted to return to the salon and lob the dregs of your glass at your hairdresser's head!

CRISIS:

It's five o'clock (at least somewhere), you're feeling hot, your skin looks great, and you want to meet some men! You've made a hundred calls, begging every friend in the book to head out for a cocktail . . . all to no avail. It figures that the night you're itching to go out you'd get stuck in the proverbial "all dressed up with nowhere to go" predicament. The normally cheesy Woo Woo is your only recourse: Consider it a one-woman party in a glass.

COCKTAIL: *Woo Woo*

1 oz. vodka
1 oz. peach schnapps
3 oz. cranberry juice
Lemon wedge

Mix all three ingredients
in a highball glass with
ice. Garnish with a lemon
wedge. Bonus points for
going to a bar yourself and
leisurely enjoying your cocktail
solo—you never know who
you could meet!

CRISIS:

You channeled Martha Stewart, put on an apron, and spent all day slaving over a gourmet, home-cooked meal for your man. In the homestretch you got caught up watching *Oprah* (Brad Pitt was talking about Angelina—who could blame you?) . . . and your delectable creation burned to an unsalvageable crisp in the oven. Since neither of you will be eating dinner, you might as well pour two tall glasses of Guinness: It's a meal in a glass.

Cocktail Therapy

(Plus, as the old slogan used to say, "Guinness is good for you"—it's loaded with iron and cancer-fighting antioxidants, which are a girl's best friends.)

COCKTAIL: *Guinness*

Although beer is usually one of those drinks you can't screw up, there is actually a lot of technique required to pour the ideal pint of Guinness stout. According to the beer's website, it takes exactly 119.5 seconds to pour the perfect pint. But, the company assures you (and we agree!), it's well worth the wait. Guinness definitely loses something when poured out of a can or bottle. So, if possible, head out to an authentic Irish pub and ask for a draft (you might also want to consider an order of oysters, the natural culinary companion to Guinness). Even better, locate a pub that just cleaned its beer taps for the purest possible Guinness experience. When we worked at an Irish bar that served Guinness on tap, we learned it tastes infinitely better coming from a clear pipe with no buildup. There's nothing wrong with asking the bartender how long it's been since the pipes have been cleaned—especially if he's cute!

CRISIS:

While focusing on getting rid of the bags under your eyes, you accidentally dropped your cell phone . . . in the toilet. Since you're not going to be talking to anyone for a while, why not whip yourself up a Silent Night? Although normally reserved for the holiday season, this cocktail can't help but make a relaxing—and conversation-free— evening alone that much more pleasant.

COCKTAIL: *Silent Night*

> 2 oz. brandy
> *(or you can try the rich cognac B & B, which has cinnamon undertones)*
> Splash of premium dark rum
> Cinnamon stick
> Grated nutmeg

Serve neat in a rocks glass. Garnish with a cinnamon stick and a pinch of grated nutmeg.

BONUS: Cinnamon has a long history as both a spice and a medicine. It's an anti-inflammatory, an antimicrobial, good for the heart, helps control blood sugar, and boosts brain function.

TIP JAR: To make this drink even more satisfying in the wintertime, pop the whole thing into the microwave for about 30

seconds, curl up on the couch, and turn off your phone. Oops! No need for that last part!

CRISIS:

You wake up confused and disoriented and glance at the clock, which reads 9:23 a.m. Shit! Your alarm clock never rang, and today just happens to be the day on which your company's monthly staff meeting is held. At 9:00 a.m.! Your lateness makes you feel off-kilter all day, and the only thing that will set your screwy day straight is a Screwdriver.

COCKTAIL: *Screwdriver*

2 oz. premium vodka
3 oz. orange juice
Orange slice

Combine and serve over ice. Garnish with the orange slice. Boost it up: Also garnish with some St. John's wort, which is said to regulate moods and decrease the blues and anxiety. At the very least, you'll benefit from the placebo effect!

TIP JAR: Fresh-squeezed juices *always* taste better than juice out of the carton. If you can get your hands on some fresh-squeezed OJ (lots of grocery stores now carry it, or you can buy a really affordable juicer and make it yourself), it will make your day that much sunnier!

CRISIS:

It's every woman's worst nightmare: You get your period a day early and are completely unprepared. No more discussion (because, seriously, who really wants to talk about it?). After locating a tampon, stat, conjure up a Blood Orange Martini to commemorate the disaster that almost was.

COCKTAIL: *Blood Orange Martini*

> 2 oz. orange-flavored vodka
> 1 oz. Campari
> 2 oz. orange juice
> Splash of cranberry juice
> Orange slice

Shake all ingredients in a shaker with ice and then pour into a chilled martini glass. Serve straight up and garnish with an orange slice.

 TIP JAR: If you can actually get your hands on some blood oranges, by all means, substitute freshly squeezed blood orange juice for the orange and cranberry juices. Blood oranges are bursting with fresh sweetness, but they tend to be very seasonal and difficult to locate.

CRISIS:

You lost your wallet and feel like your world is
crumbling to the ground. Who knew losing a
few little pieces of plastic could cause so much
trauma in a person's life? To make matters
worse, your bank just called to say that some
jerk in the next state is already trying to use
said pieces of plastic to buy himself a 1969
Harley! Take a deep breath and remember
that the old adage is true: Money can't buy
happiness, and everything material can be
replaced. Then call the last friend you bought
a drink for, request a return on that favor, and
have her meet you at your favorite watering
hole. It's just your sanity that's on the line, so
order an Amaretto Sour, the quintessential

drink that's both sweet and sour, symbolizing the good and bad side to every situation.

COCKTAIL: Amaretto Sour

2 oz. amaretto
3 oz. homemade sour mix
(see "Cheat Sheet")
Plump maraschino cherry

Combine both ingredients over ice. Garnish with the cherry.

Recipe Index

Authors *Leanne Shear* and *Tracey Toomey* met behind the bar, when they were both struggling to establish themselves in creative professions. Many years—and countless good times—later, they remain coauthors, business partners, and best friends. Visit them at www.theperfectmanhattan.com and www.whiskychicks.com.

Notes ....

....

....